WHO NEEDS GOD?

WHO NEEDS GOD?

Barbara Stöckl in conversation with
Christoph Cardinal Schönborn

Translated by Henry Taylor

IGNATIUS PRESS   SAN FRANCISCO

Original German edition:
Wer braucht Gott?
© 2007 by Ecowin Verlag, Salzburg

Cover photograph by Stefano Spaziani

Cover designed by Roxanne Mei Lum

© 2009 by Ignatius Press, San Francisco
All rights reserved
ISBN 978-1-58617-284-8
Library of Congress Control Number 2008936289
Printed in the United States of America ∞

When people stop believing in God,
they don't believe in nothing
—they believe in anything.

—Often attributed to *Gilbert Keith Chesterton*

CONTENTS

FOREWORD

The mathematician and physicist Blaise Pascal, who lived in the seventeenth century, proposed a wager with a friend as to whether there was a God or not. The friend thought there was no God. "What do I get if I win?" he asked. "Nothing", Pascal replied; "you may indeed be right, yet nonetheless you have lost. And I, too. If there is no God, then life is empty and meaningless." "And if you win?" the friend asked. "Then we have both won", said Pascal. That, his friend said, did not answer the question as to the existence of God. "Quite so," said Pascal, "but it makes it clear that you have to decide and that this decision has consequences for your life. You have to choose between two answers that have an equal probability of being right: one answer has good consequences, and the other dreadful ones. How can you hesitate?" The friend asked, "What if I am wrong?" "That makes no difference", said Pascal; "then you have enjoyed a lovely illusion. Otherwise, you would have been choosing nothingness. That does not make anyone happy." "Then I have to believe in God?" asked the friend. "You do not have to," replied Pascal, "but it is your only chance."

Nor do I know whether there is a God. For many people, the sight of the heavens, a walk along the seashore, seeing the sunrise on a mountaintop or a baby in someone's arms is proof enough.

And yet it is not easy to believe. Christianity is full of paradoxes and even full of dreadful things. But also full of sympathetic, helpful, loving messages: a future after the end, a justice that makes up for things—lovely ideas that have a consoling effect in my life.

The questions I put to Cardinal Schönborn are based on conversations with people who are searching, as I am, and would like to believe, but are often disappointed with the Church. Why do we always feel that she does not understand us? Why does she not have a quick, up-to-date answer for many of our contemporary difficulties? Is she striving against the spirit of the age, or are we really not looking for the way to her? Why do we need our faith only when things go badly for us? And why do people so dislike anyone talking about this and find it so difficult to do so?

These conversations with Cardinal Schönborn were held in the summer of 2006, in Kirchberg am Wechsel, and in the winter at Retz, in the Weinviertel [a wine-growing area].

I would like to thank Christoph Cardinal Schönborn for his readiness to answer my questions, for his time, and for his trust.

Barbara Stöckl   August 2007

Chapter 1

The Crucial Question

1.1. What Is Your Attitude toward Religion?

We talk about everything in public, even intimate things that would be better not discussed publicly. Only not questions of belief; we have an inhibition about that, almost as if it were something obscene. What we believe and on what basis—our ultimate convictions, those elusive things that give individuals a goal in life and make sense of the whole—we sort these things out on our own, in private. And if, just for once, religious matters do break through into our secularized world, then many people act disconcerted. Why do we find it so difficult to talk about questions of belief?

Even I find it difficult. In Austria nowadays, there is almost something indecent about it. Talking in public about one's sexuality, for instance, is almost commonplace; but speaking about your own beliefs is like breaking some taboo. A little while ago, I was on a radio program where people could phone in. A lady called to say, "Cardinal, tell people that they should have the confidence to speak about their faith." I replied, "Tell me yourself: What do you mean by that?" And then she said, "I always used to be embarrassed to talk about my faith, but in recent years I have simply begun to have the confidence to do it. And I am having such good experiences with this that I would like to encourage everyone to do the same."

How did you become a Christian?

Have I already become a Christian? Saint Ignatius of Antioch, a bishop at the beginning of the second century, thus still in the apostolic age, wrote on his way to martyrdom in Rome, where he was thrown to the wild beasts in the Circus, "Now, at last I am going to become a Christian." He was a very convincing Christian with a deep faith, a bishop. If even he said that, "Now, at last I am going to become a Christian", then I, too, have to say that I have not yet become a Christian; I have been on the way for sixty-two years now.

Who is a real Christian today? When you look at all the people who call themselves Christians, even those who go to church every Sunday and then very quickly forget everything they heard there, how do you feel about that? Is everyone a Christian who calls himself a Christian?

Yes and no. Yes, I am a Christian. I am baptized, I have God's assurance that he has accepted me as his child, simply because I am his creature and still more because through baptism I have become his child in a special way. To that extent, one is right to say, "I am a Christian." It even seems to me necessary to say that today. In the time of the early Church, saying "Yes, I am a Christian" could mean a death sentence. In neighboring countries, only twenty years ago, it could mean no professional career, no university studies, economic disadvantages, even going to prison. We can, nay, should say it, even if that can be dramatic. Yet there is always the qualification: I am on the way; I am a Christian and am not yet a Christian; but I hope to be that in reality one day.

Why do you see it as so important to say that?

First, I believe our age demands more clarity. Today, we will no longer tolerate what is "wishy-washy". It is not helpful. We can no longer steal past certain fundamental questions. Franz Cardinal König (d. 2004), in his infinitely wise and lovable way, used to say until shortly before he died, that each person, sooner or later, has to ask himself: "Where do I come from?", "Where am I going?", and "What is the meaning of my life?" Not asking yourself these questions means passing your own life by. We cannot help taking a position. We cannot help but say, "I believe that life has its meaning and that I have a certain responsibility in this life." I can put these questions off, even for a very long time, yet they will catch up with me again. Then, hopefully it is not so late that I have to say, "I have lost too many years." In this respect, it is important to say that I am a Christian or a Moslem or even that I do not belong to any religion, but my basic principles are these . . .

But do I necessarily have to belong to some faith community for my beliefs? Must I have a religion in order to believe?

No one can walk his path in life alone. I cannot believe on my own, nor can I live alone, without beliefs. For I am always associated with some community. The primary cell of any community is one's own family. I always have a mother, a father, grandparents, maybe brothers and sisters, children, grandchildren. I am embedded in this network of primal relationships, without which none of us would exist. And that is why I can never say that I am completely alone in believing or that I live without beliefs, without religion, entirely alone, for myself. I always stand in relationships, in the exchange of ideas. Unfortunately, prejudices that I share with others, prejudices with which I grew up, was raised, and from which perhaps I rid myself so as to arrive at conscious beliefs of my own, are also a part of that. Then I realize that I am not alone even in these beliefs. I look for people with whom I can stand up for these convictions. A community is formed with them—whether it is a large religious community like a church, like a worldwide religion, or just a small community of interests. I cannot believe alone and cannot live alone without beliefs.

1.2. Is It Possible Not to Believe? Atheism in the Twentieth and Twenty-first Centuries

Is it possible not to believe at all?

No. Belief is in the first instance a fundamental attitude of trust. Whenever I sit down in the train, I naturally trust that the cars and the engine are in working order, that the engineer is performing his job properly and the safety systems are functioning. If I added up how much trust I advance to everyone! Our whole life can actually function only on the basis of a fundamental trust. We see that as if in a distorting mirror when people have a persecution complex. Without a basic trust in the people I meet, it becomes impossible to live. If I regard everyone as a criminal, then I can no longer go out on the street—but neither can I stay at home. Actually, I cannot live at all. So belief is absolutely a part of everyone's life.

Believing is, again, a fundamental human attitude: the trust of a child in his parents, the trust of spouses in each other, the trust in economic relations. That is why it is so enormously painful when a relationship of trust is damaged or even destroyed—of children toward their parents, spouses in one another, or business relations—when we are betrayed. That hurts so much because we are constructed on trust and on good faith. The entire legal basis of our society in Austria—of every society—is founded on the principle of faith and trust.

Of course, that is not everything—that is merely the human plane. Can you live without belief in God? Of course you can. There are many people who do that; from not having seriously thought about it, because it has not confronted them on their way through life. In the former East Germany, up to 80 percent of people are not baptized and have virtually never heard anything about religion. Respectable, hardworking people may be among them. Whether that is enough, in the long term, I doubt. Human experience, over thousands of years, has shown that religion is a fundamental dimension of man. *Religio*—literally, being connected to God—has been a part of mankind from the beginning. In research into the early history of man, so-called paleontology, you begin to talk about "man" with certainty when you find burial objects and traces of formal burial. That is to say, when you can say: Here we have a religious belief in an afterlife and, thus, in another life besides the one on this earth. Therefore, a belief in God. Seen as part of the history of mankind, the history of atheism, as the phenomenon that developed in Europe since the eighteenth century, since the Enlightenment, is an exception. I would almost say, something like a brief parenthesis in the long history of mankind. Religion has always been a part of man; man is a religious being and will continue to be so in the future. I also have the impression that in recent decades, religion has been making a comeback worldwide. That has been a serious concern to a lot of people. How is it coming back, in what form? One thing is certain, at any rate: religion is a fundamental phenomenon of human life.

The Archdiocese of Cologne has distributed cards with the text, "Tell us about your life without God", asking what atheists think. The result was that many people sent in replies in which their wrestling and searching for answers were noticeable. These people are probably closer to God than many others who would describe themselves as believers.

I believe we have to accept the possibility of a conscious, deliberate, and clear atheism. God—and I speak as someone who believes—has given us the freedom for that. He has given us the freedom even to say, "I don't need you"; even the freedom to say, "You don't exist." That reminds me of a saying of my first spiritual director, Pater Paulus, who said to me when I was an adolescent and had rebelled against more or less everything, "Even if you said to me one day, 'You cannot like me', I will still like you." It is a little bit like that with God. He says that to us, too. Fundamentally, you have to accept that there is this possibility. I am thinking of the book by the sociologist Norbert Elias that I read years ago. He says quite clearly and unequivocally that everything is over at death. He simply does not believe that there is anything else. And he led a model life, an interesting and decent life. Therefore, I would not dare to say that you cannot live without God. I do not know.

For my own part, I can say that I cannot imagine a life without faith. In my youth, I did once give it a try, at least to some extent, in that difficult year of '67, when the student revolt was at its climax in Germany—I was twenty-two years old, then. Although I was in a monastery—that was the time of the great crisis, when everything was in disorder and confused—I did really try not to pray for a year. Some people explicitly maintained the theory that prayer is pointless. You have to act. My big idea then, at the age of twenty-two, was social action. I committed myself with enthusiasm, entirely and wholly, to the homeless, alcoholics, and all kinds of social concerns. But for a year, I did not pray. Which means I probably did pray, but I was trying to leave it out. And the astonishing thing, for me, was that I found nothing missing to begin with. You almost feel a little bit liberated, and you believe that is freedom, no longer being constrained to get up early for communal prayers, having the rhythm, the obligations, and also the effort of prayer. Only then, as the months went by, I noticed that things were becoming imperceptibly more and more gray. They had lost their contrast and color. I do not know how that would have gone on if I had not at that time received a really great grace. I can recall the time and place, exactly. It was by a stained-glass window by Alfred Wickenburg in the chapel of Schloss Seggau, the cultural center of the Diocese of Graz. It was a new vocation. It was in the season of Easter, and I believe I can say that the Lord called me back again.

So he liked me, even when I said to him, "You cannot like me." I am very grateful for that; it could have turned out quite differently. Faith could simply have faded away. Through non-use, a certain practiced ability diminishes. If you simply do not use a certain organ of your body, then it atrophies. Thus the vein of religion, the life of faith, can atrophy. And in the end, the barrier to return is so high you can no longer get over it. It then seems to you like a wall. Behind that something is taking place that you are no longer acquainted with, something that has become alien to you.

Do you often have discussions with atheists?

Previously more than now. People probably do not have enough confidence to say to a bishop that they are atheists. So I have less opportunity to do so. Now, in the course of the debate about evolution, I again had the opportunity to talk with the scientist Renée Schroeder, who declared this to me.

And there is a book by you about this question. In America, there is a new atheistic movement as a counter movement to the close relations between religion and politics. It is led by biologist Richard Dawkins, who talks about "God delusion" and says that he will leave believers in peace if they leave us and our children in peace and if they stop fighting among themselves and putting our world in danger. His book The God Delusion *was a best-seller. Is the pendulum swinging the other way?*

Richard Dawkins certainly cannot be regarded as representative of the scientific community. He is a successful writer, a provocative author, but not a truly significant man in the scientific community.

Richard Dawkins is referred to by many people as one of the most important evolutionary biologists and was voted one of the three most important intellectuals in the world. And other critical thinkers, like the French philosopher Michel Onfray or the Italian mathematician Piergiorgio Odifreddi, have recently made public statements. Why We Cannot be Christians is the title of Odifreddi's book. Is there a new scientific opposition to the Catholic view of the world?

Dawkins has since become a fanatical preacher of atheism, in a kind of new, antichristian fundamentalism. And there are other researchers who associate their findings with a world view that is at times even militantly atheistic or critical of religion.

What is much more exciting is what is being done at the moment in research on the brain. But actually, in all spheres of research, through the ever greater discovery of the extreme complexity and, above all, the incredible synergy of all things, which can be seen at all levels, people are arriving at models quite different from that of Darwin. I am thinking, for instance, of the new book by the Freiburg neurobiologist Joachim Bauer: *The Principle of Humanity: Why We Naturally Cooperate*—who says that the Darwinian model of a struggle for existence is not sustainable scientifically. The basic pattern in nature is synergy. That can be shown right down to small details in research into the brain. Man is dependent on cooperation, and that is equally true of lower forms of life. The struggle for existence is one element, but it is by no means the most decisive or influential. What has much greater force is interdependence and cooperation, to the point of compassion. Based on the evidence of the latest neurological research, Joachim Bauer suggests that man is formed and conceived entirely with others in view.

Was it not predictable that a backlash would inevitably arise?

We in Europe do not have to take part in this swing of the pendulum, since the one extreme is just as wrong as the other. So-called creationism, which is supported by certain evangelical circles, is absurd—that is, maintaining that the world is six thousand years old and that creation happened in six days—because it is literally so in the Bible. This way of understanding the Bible is certainly not the Catholic one, and that is why this swing of the pendulum is out of the question for us. And we will never argue that this ought to be taught in schools. It is utterly nonsense. Yet, on the other hand, the crude atheistic theories of someone like Richard Dawkins are just as unscientific.

Yet the atheist movement does seem to have reached Europe. Ought not the Church to give this some thought?

Atheism actually started its unholy career in Europe. It has nothing to do with science. Any more than does creationism, which makes the further mistake of thinking it can be scientifically demonstrated that the world is only six thousand years old. We are in the realm of absurdities, there. On the other hand, the assertion that you can prove atheism scientifically is as false as Marxism's attempt to construct a "scientific atheism". That is a confessional question, a question of belief, which should be kept out of science. You have to separate science from world view. Dawkins, for instance, does not make this distinction.

Professor Anton Zeilinger, the quantum physicist, wrote in a recent article that he would like more tolerance on both sides; only then would the discussion get anywhere.

Yes. Whereas we have to assert energetically that if we support belief in creation, we are not thereby creationists. I definitely believe, on rational grounds, that there is a Creator. There are certainly good reasons for believing that, even if not scientific ones. I cannot prove this mathematically, but with my reason, which is greater than mathematics, which goes beyond what can be mathematically quantified, I can very well say: The order that I find in nature, from the atom to the galaxy, which I find everywhere in living things, this order says something about someone who establishes order, this design says something about a designer, or this plan something about a planner.

Then why are you always being associated with creationists?

That is a simpler way of dealing with this, by which people do not need to give serious consideration to belief in a Creator. They were already trying that in the summer of 2005, when I wrote an article ("Finding Design in Nature") in the *New York Times* and gave an interview. The editor tried to change the text I had written. I opposed this and said, "That is not my position; I am not a creationist. I believe in creation, but not that it is only six thousand years old. I am not at all afraid of the results of natural science. But—and I make this distinction clearly—I am convinced that for anyone engaged in accurate and honest scientific research, the inner, intellectual space is opened for the question that wonders, "Who is behind it? Who made it, and how?" "Two things", as Immanuel Kant (d. 1804) said, fill me with "wonder and awe": "The starry heaven above me and the moral law within me." In these things I perceive the Creator. And the order in nature speaks to me of someone who establishes order.

Richard Dawkins writes that what he would like to ask a God, if there is one, is why he is so intent on our believing in him.

I take this question to be a gag. It is not a serious question. I should like, in turn, to put a question to Richard Dawkins. In an interview in which I had the honor of being personally abused by him, he said that he would not like to live in a Darwinian world. For a Darwinian world, he said, would be a fascist one. I should like to put this question to Dawkins: How can he escape from a Darwinian world if everything is evolution? Where does he get the freedom to turn against the mainstream of Darwinism in nature? Has "evolution" given him the freedom to emancipate himself from it? Where does he get the freedom to act in any other way but according to the Darwinian laws of nature? I would like to have an answer from him to this question.

1.3. How Does One Become Religious?

The longing for religion—being connected (Latin, religari) with some origin—for something all-inclusive, possibly something holy, cannot be excluded from this world. In any case, this longing is manifested, not necessarily in a belief in religious dogmas, but in an individual search for meaning: in climbing mountains, in the esoteric scene, or in Far Eastern religions. For what does a person need faith, and how can I find it? Is faith not ultimately a question of education, in the first instance, of socialization?

Faith is very much something that is handed on, that is true. We almost always see that in the testimony given by people who believe. I know hardly a single exception among those people who have recounted the story of their life to me or about whom I have read. There is hardly anyone who believes who has not arrived at his faith either through an education in faith in his own family or through meeting other people who believe. That has certainly always been, and still is, the great strength of a family in which faith is alive. For when you experience your parents as believers, in faith, then you quite naturally identify with this very early. And if that faith is not a pretense, not "put on", but authentic, then it makes a deep impression on the children. That is certainly the best way of handing on faith.

Here is one example that I will never forget: I was celebrant when a young woman received the habit as a Dominican. I was not yet a bishop then, but, as a Dominican father, was authorized to officiate at this clothing, thus to receive her into the order. In our preparatory conversation, I asked her, "Tell me about some religious experience in your youth or childhood that left a deep impression." Then she told me the following: her parents had a carpentry business, her father was a coffin maker—I knew her parents, in a small town in the Vorarlberg—and as a little girl, she once rushed into her parents' bedroom, late in the evening, without knocking. And she found her parents both kneeling by their bed in prayer. She said that made an unforgettable impression—"My parents pray! Not in front of us, to show us, but together, kneeling before God."

In my youth as a student, I studied psychology a bit, and I have continued to take an interest in the subject. In doing so, I have come to the conclusion that the father-son and mother-daughter relationships that figure so largely in modern literature—Kafka, Strindberg, and so on—and which Sigmund Freud (d. 1939) defined as the "Oedipus complex", is decisively changed if the children experience their parents as people who share their faith. It is of course at least as important that they should experience each other as people who love. Yet if children experience their parents as believers, then there is never a danger of parental authority becoming inflated, as in Freud's Oedipus complex. For the children experience their parents as authority, which they are, yet at the same time as children before God, so to speak, which in turn relativizes their authority in a good sense. If everyone kneels down before God together, then the authoritative position of the parents vis-à-vis the children is in a certain sense mitigated by the counterbalancing effect of standing before God together and being sustained by God. People who were fortunate enough to have this experience—I am not among them—have a strong foundation for their "religious socialization".

But when you yourself say that you did not have a religious upbringing, that also shows that there are quite different paths to faith.

Yes. There are other paths. Yet they too have to do with examples, even if not provided by the parents. For me, it was above all one priest, and then other priest figures, and also relations in our extended family. These were people in whom, as a child, or as a youth, I perceived a deep and persuasive faith—not something "put on", not a pretense, but a faith that was consistent both inwardly and outwardly. What certainly does not help religious socialization is anything that is put-on or forced.

What exactly do you mean by "put-on", and "forced"?

Many people of a certain generation in Austria have difficulties with their education in a monastery or convent, because they had the feeling—sometimes rightly, sometimes wrongly—that these religious authorities, sisters, monks, and priests, were not credible. There was too much that was authoritarian and too little genuine authority.

Many people suffered quite dreadful injustice that way. Many who had a convent education or were in a Catholic boarding-school report it as the worst time of their lives.

Whether people actually remember it as it is then described is another question. Sometimes, I venture to suspect that there may also be a certain element of self-justification for no longer taking one's religion seriously. But I have found, time and again, that people have been traumatized by a failed religious upbringing.

What is a religious upbringing? Are very naïve images a part of that? Are they important or right or even dangerous?

What is important, is that they should be the right images. But what are the right images? I am convinced that the Bible offers us an incomparable treasure trove of images, figures, and symbols that can shape the landscape of a soul. That is an idea I have pondered for years, but I have had far too little time to follow it up personally. And there must be many clever people who have reflected on how deeply the inner landscape of Europe has been influenced by these powerful images in the Bible.

Especially in the church year in which we have readings from the Gospel of Luke, I recall the following story: a few years ago, in an ecumenical celebration with the Evangelical superintendent, I blessed the operational center of the Arbeiter Samariter Bund in Vienna. I was pleased and surprised that an association belonging to the Social-Democratic camp asked the archbishop to bless their operational center. The name, "Workers' Samaritan Federation", reminds us of a figure from the Bible, the Good Samaritan. It is moving to see how this image from the Bible has lent a name to an organization that is not in the first instance closely associated with the Church. The fact that they chose this name shows me how this parable of Jesus, the story of the Good Samaritan, has left an impression on the inner landscape for centuries. Generations of people have identified themselves with this image and have found in it their motivation not to pass by someone in need but to be a real neighbor to them, as Jesus said.

I believe that these great biblical images have made a much more profound impression on Europe than we generally assume. One might mention the parable of the Prodigal Son, the crib at Bethlehem—a subject that has been taken up a million times with variations, always inspiring—and above all, the image of the crucified Jesus. And likewise the images from the Old Testament, which we Catholics unfortunately often do not know as well as the Evangelical Christians, such as the story of Joseph: Joseph and his brothers, Joseph in Egypt, the story of David, the story of the fall of man in Paradise.

All that sounds like a very childish religion. How important is it for an awakening faith, or one that is already awake, to know that those are all just images?

The decisive question is not, "Was it really like that?" but, "How powerful an influence do these images exercise?" There are some scenes in the Bible that can move me to tears.

Which ones, for example?

Well, for example, there is the sacrifice of Isaac. God finally grants Abraham and Sarah, in their old age—when she is already beyond the age of bearing children—the son for whom they have been longing: Isaac. Then God says to Abraham, "Take your son, and go up onto the mountain that I will show you, and offer him as a sacrifice there." They set off, with a few servants, and on the third day they see the mountain onto which they must go. They leave the servants and the donkey below. Isaac carries the wood, and Abraham the fire, and so they go up. Then comes that poignant scene which is quite briefly recounted. Isaac says, "Father!" and Abraham says, "Yes, my son?" Isaac says, "Here is the wood for the fire, but where is the sacrifice?" And then Abraham says, "God will take care of it." And they go on. The drama of this brief dialogue between the son, who has no idea what lies before him, and the father, who does know but does not have the heart to say it to his son, is incomparably moving.

And there is another scene that particularly affects me, David's mourning for Absalom. Absalom, one of David's many sons, has risen against the king in his old age and has instigated a civil war—a classic scenario. David has to flee from Jerusalem under humiliating circumstances. Then comes the decisive battle. David says explicitly, "Spare Absalom for me!" The King's general, his military leader, catches Absalom in an oak forest and runs him through with several spears. David is sitting in the gate of the city to which he has fled, and he sees a runner coming, and a second one. He says, "That is a good sign." The first question he puts to the messenger is, "How is it with Absalom?" He replies, "May it be for all the king's enemies as it is for Absalom." At that, David goes up into the tower and weeps bitterly and calls out again and again, "Absalom, my son Absalom!" And it says farther on, "On this day, Israel was in mourning, as after a defeat." That is one of the classic scenes from the Bible, which are presented with extreme concision. There is not one word too many, but an incredible emotional intensity. The figure of King David, which determined the image of a king all through the Middle Ages, makes a deep impression on the spiritual landscape.

A third example, which always moves me profoundly, is Peter's denial in the house of the high priest, as Luke portrays it. Only he recounts how Jesus turned round at that moment, and looked at Peter. Nothing is added as commentary there; it says only: "He looked at him." And Peter goes out and weeps bitterly. There you perceive that the Bible is also a great school of human feelings, of sorrow, pain, joy, of moments of truth.

To get back to children: What makes me so sad about religious education today, even in our religious books, is the fact that often people obviously do not believe that these strong biblical images can make the powerful impression they actually do.

Are not many of the biblical images very brutal, perhaps too brutal for children?

And yet as children we enthusiastically heard or read Grimm's fairy tales, and they are very brutal. There is a dreadful lot of brutality in the world. Children see this when they watch the news every day. And the brutality in the Bible is much less harmful than the violence you can see nowadays in every thriller or in computer games. But all this is set in a context where evil really is evil, and the victory over evil really is the victory over evil. In this respect, one can only encourage children to approach the Bible.

Many people in Austria say about themselves that they had a religious, Catholic upbringing, but then afterward something happened. As soon as people grow up, there are so many "careless" Catholics, spoiled Christians—that seems to me to be the prevailing course for faith in Austria. Is it merely a matter of people beginning to think, to question things, to doubt—will their faith not tolerate any reason?—or what is happening here?

I have noticed that even in the innermost sphere of the Church. It usually goes all right up to fourteen. Recently it has sometimes begun to happen earlier. If there has been a certain religious start in life at home, if there has been some introduction to faith at home. If that is not the case, then there is a different situation again, which I would quite openly call neo-pagan, not at all in a pejorative sense, but simply stating the case. That would have to be dealt with in its own way. But let us first take those families in which, let us say, there is at least a certain traditional religious character. It is fairly certain that that will stop after confirmation. So that up to 90 percent, I believe, are no longer to be seen after confirmation.

Ninety percent—surely that is a very high percentage?

Yes. Many of them, of course, were not to be seen even before, and then they turned up for confirmation and went away again. But I certainly believe that puberty has a strong effect. That was mitigated somewhat, in earlier times, by a stronger social framework and also by the social sanctions that existed in society. It now breaks out quite violently. I believe that is simply, for many young people, a time of life when they cannot make very much of the Church or of religion. Probably because they have to find themselves.

I am concerned about the time of life that Sigmund Freud called the "latency period". That is a time when people should hold off on sexual relations and should get to know themselves. I sometimes have the impression that the latency period is being short-circuited by the way young people live together nowadays, by living together in partnership far too early, often as young as fourteen. And actually, what Freud had quite correctly observed is missing here: going through this period of waiting—I am not yet grown up, but I am no longer a child; I have to conquer the world for myself, get to know it, and get to know the opposite sex, the curiosity that is a part of all this, experiencing all the differences, why I am like this, and why a girl is different, the process of approaching one another, without this being short-circuited sexually, so to speak. I believe this widespread disappearance of the latency period makes coming to maturity, and also successful partnerships, very much more difficult.

What does that imply for faith? Do I need to be equipped in childhood so that then I can retrieve it later? Or does it mean that everything from childhood has gone, and we have to start over again after this time?

Many do have the chance to pick up the thread of what they experienced as children. But I find that this often happens very much later, when people's own children are coming to the phase of religious socialization, so that the question of religion is opened up again through the children. But I certainly believe that in the youth culture of today, it has become more difficult to live through this process of maturing, which we must all undergo, in a more clear and better defined way. That is why we have this strange phenomenon of people finding it so difficult to decide to get married, despite having lived together earlier. People are much less happy about making decisions—which does not mean that the partnerships do not hold together for years, often very well. Yet the real commitment, which one makes before all society and before God—"We belong together, and we will stay together"—that is made much later. There are of course also economic reasons for this, and it is part of the general trend of society. I believe, however, that it is also because this latency period in youth has largely ceased to exist.

1.4. Cafeteria Religion, Spirituality, and Esotericism

What you get in the end is what sociologists call "cafeteria religion". To the extent trust in churches, political parties, and labor unions disappears, the individual has to determine his own identity. So people take a bit of religion, a bit of Christian teaching, a bit of Buddhism, a bit of the esoteric, a bit of nature, and a bit of sporting spirit, and they cobble something together for themselves with which they feel actually very good and sustained through the life to come—love of one's neighbor with incense sticks. What do you think of this modern approach to the subject of religion?

It is the kind of approach you find in many other spheres of life today: people put things together. It is part of a contemporary trend—I find it quite alarming that even our careers have become a patchwork. When I came of age in 1963, the matter-of-course-prospect was: you chose a career, you studied—law or economics, for example—you got a job, perhaps in the firm for which your parents were already working, and then you had a job for life, up to retirement, and you could safely take things for granted and proceed to build a house, start a family, and so on. Who can do that today? Young people? Place of work and place of residence change much more often than they used to. Who, nowadays, has employment that will last the rest of his life? Not even official tenure seems to survive in the long run.

And there are economic reasons for that, in the first place—for young people, that kind of security no longer exists; they are glad in the beginning to find a position as trainee or any kind of job. Having a career, and one that corresponds to your own calling, is far too rare. Yet, on the other hand, there is also a positive side to showing how versatile you are, not getting stale in one job, which perhaps never was the right one. Always having to question yourself anew, reorient yourself, prove yourself over again, discover your real strengths and abilities, being able to learn, to search, and to realize yourself all your life—all that can also be very enriching?

A different attitude to life is needed—one that, as always in life, certainly has its good and its not so good sides, and that has indeed come about: that is how it is today. But the result is that in all probability the coming generations will be worse off economically than ours. And with greater flexibility in every sphere of life, there will always be the question: Where is my own place? This is actually a time that can be lived well and even creatively by people who are secure in themselves. But this inner security is not made easy for us. A patchwork family, patchwork religion, and a patchwork world of work are not necessarily what we need to give us a feeling of being at ease in ourselves, a firm base, a strong backbone, and a confident approach to life; on the contrary, it creates a good deal of emotional insecurity, homelessness. I see here a very important task for the community of faith—I am quite deliberately not saying "the Church"—so that people can find a framework there that is not a patchwork and does not function only by sections; something that offers a fixed, solid home, a "roof over the soul", as Paul Michael Zulehner calls it. I am not surprised that the number of people who are not merely coming back to the Church, but discovering her for the first time, is steadily growing. I believe more and more people are feeling, in this patchwork situation, that somewhere they need a place where they can find a certain kind of solidity, for themselves and also for the framework of their life, for their life-style.

Yet these developments are clearly moving in opposite directions: more and more people are looking for faith and are taking an interest in questions of belief, even in religion and in paths to faith—and at the same time, more and more people are leaving the Church, so not finding there the "roof for the soul" of which you were just talking. That must give you food for thought?

That gives us all much to think about. I believe it is not primarily a matter of there being scandals in the Church. On this subject, of people leaving the Church, there is a distressing observation. The great wave of departures began at the end of the seventies and the beginning of the eighties. Before that, the numbers were much smaller, and then they shot up and stayed high virtually until now. What is striking about it is that in those years in which there were scandals, there were spikes in the number leaving. Yet these peaks are not remarkably higher than the base level. The alarming thing is that the base number of people leaving the Church each year, independently of particular events, even in the years when Pope John Paul II (d. 2005) was right at the height of his popularity, in the early years of his pontificate, and Cardinal König was Archbishop of Vienna— the number leaving was just as high then as now.

Why is that? I believe the reason is that people definitely value personal qualities. Cardinal König and Pope John Paul II were extraordinarily popular. People found them fabulous, first-rate, super, simply persuasive. Yet that did not rub off on the institution, and this is true today. Individual people have a great popularity value. The institution of the Church as such is very little affected by that. What should we conclude from this? I believe the main reason is the strong deterioration of the traditional bond. Why is the number of those leaving the Church at the highest in the big city of Vienna?

When someone comes to Vienna from Upper Austria, from Lower Austria, Burgenland, Styria, or the Tyrol, the traditional bond simply disappears. Leaving the Church in a village has a different significance from what it has in a big city.

Is the significance of religion in the country different from what it is in a city? Is faith still alive there, whereas it dies away in many people through urbanization and isolation?

Fundamentally, that is true. But meanwhile, something is happening that once again gives cause for reflection. Even the traditional bonds in village communities are swiftly dwindling. That, too, has social reasons, such as the disappearance of the rural farming community, which has practically been reduced to a minimum over the past thirty or forty years. Our country parishes around Vienna are commuter parishes; in the broad sense they have become suburbs of Vienna. That means that all the traditional religious bonds have simply become very much looser. And if you once stop going to church for any length of time, then the threshold to be crossed in returning is too high. Something special has to happen for people to have the confidence to venture over the threshold again and find a new avenue of approach. You need a powerful personal religious experience for that. Then you can find the courage again. Otherwise, the Church becomes increasingly foreign for you, and you do not feel comfortable stepping into a church.

Yet urbanization and the disappearance of traditional bonds are not the only reasons for people leaving the Church. The subject is stirring people—indeed, an entire generation of seekers is growing up and obviously finding better answers in the shape of cafeteria religion than the Church has to offer. Other religious communities, too, are "modern"; movements like that of esotericism in the wider sense attract young people. What is the Church missing? Does she speak the wrong language? Why is Buddhism so chic, or does it simply make things easier for people? Are people finding the answers in a better form in esotericism, one that is easier to consume, to understand?

I believe at least one reason for other religions' power of attraction is the lack of obligations. It is something else again to live in a Buddhist environment such as Sri Lanka. I am somewhat familiar with it and have visited people there. In a society in which three-quarters of the population are Buddhists, the religion, together with its way of life, also makes demands. In our society, Buddhism is something interesting, but it is still very intellectual . . .

Exotic, making no demands, and yet for many more contemporary, more free and liberal, not so rigid and outmoded as the Catholic Church seems to many.

And also somewhat fashionable. By that I do not mean to say that those among us who take this path do not intend to do it honestly, personally, and also seriously. But I do think they should then also have the courage to have a look at what it is like in practice, if this religion is actually being lived in a binding way. I have to make a decision to commit myself in my life. That is also what any good psychologist will tell you. A cafeteria religion runs the risk of being merely a reflection of my own ego, of not leading me out of myself, beyond myself.—There is the fellow from Berlin who said to another, "Man, go into yourself!"—"Been there already, there's nothing there."—You are left with yourself, turning around yourself. It is not for nothing that people talk about "ego-religion" and "ego-trip". Every religion, if it is lived seriously, demands a commitment and takes me beyond my own self. If I create my own religion for myself, then I stay with myself. That is the great danger in cafeteria religion, and by the way that is the great danger in patchwork relationships. Living out a commitment, on the other hand, is very powerful.

How do you see the influence of esotericism and everything that goes with it? Today there is an enormous, confusing market of proposals and methods, among which it is hard to discover what can really help, what "takes me beyond myself", and what only contributes to inflating the ego and the bank balance of the person offering it. Do you see spiritual help in this or a great danger?

There are two sides to esotericism. There is a genuine, authentic side and a great deal of charlatanry. It is not easy to distinguish the two. We are trying to help people tell the difference, offering someone to contact on questions of world views. It is not necessarily significant, every time you breathe on a stone. In every religion, even in Christianity, there is an esoteric—that is, an inner—dimension, which is in danger of being overlooked in "exoteric", traditional religion—that is, religion as lived externally. There have always been movements in Christianity that give more emphasis to this interior side of religion: the whole mystical tradition, the tradition of spiritual experience. And I think many people have a longing for this and find what they experience as Church—perhaps, too, because they have too superficial a knowledge of it—too external, a matter of forms, usage, and so on. Then they come across esoteric teachings, which people like to present as secret doctrines, special ways to a special experience, and there they discover a dimension they have found lacking in traditional religion. Yet I would venture to maintain that a great deal of what is offered nowadays as esoteric religion will not stand up to serious examination.

And yet esotericism seems to be well on the way to becoming a substitute religion for many people? And in the end works with many religious symbols, even Christian ones. All these mystical images—the Mother of God, angels, and so on—are they now bad in esotericism and good in Christianity? Or how should we deal with this?

Esotericism, like cafeteria religion, like patchwork situations in general, is always in danger of remaining devoid of commitment. It is in danger, one has to say quite clearly, of leading to wrong commitments. There are even entanglements in esotericism that can be psychologically very damaging. That can result in problematic dependencies, and we can see this in a sphere I do not like to talk about in public yet which certainly does exist: the whole sphere of the demonic. Getting too deeply into esotericism can lead to bad associations and dependencies, and dealing with them then brings something like a liberation. It is not for nothing that Jesus also gave his disciples the mission of setting people free from demons. That is a reality which is unfortunately widespread nowadays.

The "generation of seekers" does prefer to use the term "spirituality" instead of "religion". What is the distinction?

"Spirituality" requires no commitment. It is an entirely positive reality. It simply reminds us that, besides his material dimension, man has a spiritual one. Spirituality reminds us that man does not live by bread alone (as Jesus says), but also has to nourish his spiritual dimension in order to be human. That can come about simply by having spiritual interests—cultural, literary, musical, artistic. That includes something that may be called "religious" in a fairly broad sense.

The German comedian and entertainer Hape Kerkeling has written a book about his pilgrimage on the way of Saint James. I'm Off Then, it is called. This book has sold over two million copies, a real best-seller. So there must be something there that interests people and rouses their curiosity. Spirituality with a comedian's help.

I have not yet read the book, but it does demonstrate a religious dimension of experience that cannot be attained by itself. Hence the search for spirituality—that is, for some school, for a spiritual milieu in which one may learn from the experience of others. That is why many people in our society seek it in the Far East, in Buddhist spirituality or in Chinese wisdom. Others look for wisdom, as far as they know it, among Indians or with shamans; others, again, seek deeper in the roots of European culture, going back to the Celts. The danger in these attempts is that they are artificial, because they do not correspond to our contemporary way of life. What do we really know about Indians and their spirituality? What do we know about shamans? We live in a different world. Yet all these movements in search of something show that man does not find material things to be enough.

If the point is to go beyond oneself, perhaps it is logical to go beyond borders and look for an impulse from afar.

The most obvious thing, for us Europeans, would of course be to seek out our Christian roots. And many do try that, too. The difficulty with that spirituality is that it much more quickly becomes demanding. You can talk about shamanism in a very abstract or diffuse fashion, in an indefinite and uncommitted way, and move around in it. The same is true of Indian spirituality.

Christian spirituality has much more clearly defined contours; it has a history that is much more present, surrounding us with its historical monuments, in its concrete forms, and even in its very practical demands. That is why I always say, to use a Buddhist image, that spirituality is like a boat. Buddhism distinguishes between a large and a small vessel. The image of passage is a primal image for life. We are crossing from the land of our prenatal situation, or our origin, across the sea of life, to a land to come, to eternal life. We need a boat for the crossing. Swimming alone is not enough. We could not manage it.

The great danger right now for Europeans, as I see it, is that they want to jump to and fro between various boats, a little while here and a little while there. The crossing cannot succeed like that. Whoever gets into a boat has committed himself. He has only that boat, he has the crew, and he is, for better or for worse, dependent on that boat. If someone quite clearly decides in favor of one path, and if it is that of Buddhism, and then follows that path completely and concretely and with commitment, I have to say that I have great respect for him, even though that is not my path. Hence, spirituality is necessary and good, yet a great deal of nonsense, and even some dangerous things, may hide behind the name of spirituality.

1.5. Where Is God?

You have said that the way back to faith or the way to faith at all can only be by way of some powerful religious experience. What is a powerful religious experience?

There are powerful religious experiences that are not necessarily an experience of faith—a powerful experience of nature, for example. There is a good example of this that occurs quite often in Russian literature. Unfortunately, I have not yet experienced it myself. The impression, when you suddenly see the Caucasus rising up out of the steppe in the south of Russia, must be overwhelming. Nikolai Gogol (d. 1852) writes about it, as does Alexander Solzhenitsyn, and for Sergei Bulgakov (d. 1944) it was the beginning of his conversion. This tremendous experience of one of the wonders of nature can be a powerful religious experience. The shock of a death, of a great pain or sorrow, even an intense experience of love can all become a great shock in religious terms, a religious experience. It might be an inner experience: suddenly silence becomes tangible, the presence of God becomes perceptible. I would describe all that as religious experience. Julien Green (d. 1998), the Franco-American writer, has described in his religious autobiography a scene in which, as a child, alone in his room at night at the age of five, he suddenly had an overwhelming experience of a presence he could not name. He said only that this had been with him for the rest of his life. And only later, when he had found faith, was he able to call this an experience of God that he had had as a child. Those are religious experiences.

How does that differ from an experience of faith?

I would distinguish an experience of faith from a religious experience by its being associated with the demand of being addressed by the divine "Thou", a vocation experience, for example. I remember the moment, at the age of eleven, when my vocation to be a priest first came to me. That is an experience of faith, in contrast to a religious experience. Why a faith experience? Because it is directly linked with a demand, with a particular call, and quite clearly and unambiguously a "Thou". That is surely most clearly expressed in the experience of vocation.

It is exactly for this decisive experience that many searching people are waiting, what they are missing so much. If I have made the basic decision to believe in God, the question still remains: Where is he! Where is he, today? Where can I find him in our world?

I think it is essential here to excavate a virtue or a concept we have timidly buried in ecclesiastical discourse. People feel embarrassed to mention it nowadays, but it is there in the Bible on every page—the term "fear of God". That is not being afraid of God, such as we see everywhere in pagan religions, in which you have to appease the gods with sacrifices. It concerns religious experiences, the *tremendum*, being frightened before the Divine or also the fascination of the Divine. In the Old Testament, fear of God is explicitly said to be a gift of the Holy Spirit—at every confirmation, I pray that the young people may receive the sevenfold gifts of the Holy Spirit and, thus, the gift of the fear of God. I see fear of God as a kind of fright at the incomprehensibility of God. Just as you said, "Where is he?" The older I get, the more often the question comes to me: Where is he? Who is he? God is quite certainly not an anonymous energy, as is often said: "I believe in a higher power." His is a frightening, incomprehensible reality that is very close and very mysterious, that is absolutely, unconditionally a "Thou". I would describe this as a closeness greater than any closeness I can imagine, and at the same time an incomprehensible something beyond.

1.6.   The Usefulness of Religion: Who Needs God?

Now, we live in a world that is very much usefulness- and result-oriented. Can these criteria also be applied to faith; does that get us anywhere? "Who needs God?" is the title of this book, and that already suggests: What do I get out of it? What use is faith to me, what are the results, what advantage does it bring me?

That is by no means wrong. The Gospels are full of quite utilitarian and profit-oriented considerations. Jesus is quite unashamed about the images he uses, parables from everyday life. "Make friends for yourself by means of unrighteous mammon", he says. Religion is very useful. For Jesus, it is foolish not to be religious or to be without faith. There was a man who reaped an enormous harvest. He wondered, "What shall I do? I will tear down my barn and build a bigger one, and then I will have plenty set aside for years ahead and I can lie in the sun"—and that is, "Soul, take your ease", he says. "You fool!" God then says to him, "This night God will require your life from you, and then what will you have of all this?" It is definitely, verifiably useful to think about these questions.

Yet what would you say was the use of believing, the usefulness of religion?

Helmut Qualtinger (d. 1986) used to sing, "I don't know where I'm going, but that only means I'll get there faster!" I know where I am going; never mind when I will get there, but I do know where I am going. I know that my life has a goal, that a period of time has been allotted me, that I have received this time as a gift and should make the wisest possible use of it. I know I can be confident, even God is looking out for me. Many years ago, when I was a young Dominican, my superior in the order once said to me, "You have such brazen confidence in God." I took that as a great compliment. Unfortunately, sometimes in difficult situations I am by no means so trusting in God, but for the most part my faith gives me a "brazen confidence in God". I know through my faith that everything will turn out well, even the most difficult situations. I am sure of it—he has promised, and he will keep it.

For whom is religion useful now and how?

There is a saying of the Apostle Paul. In the Vulgate, in Latin, it runs, "pietas ad omnia utilis est." *Pietas*, in Greek *eusebeia*, religion, is useful for everything. An ironic commentator—I think it was Étienne Gilson (d. 1978)—then expanded this, "Yes, that is true, religion is useful for everything; but", he added, "it replaces nothing." That is, religion does not replace my work or my effort or my everyday life. Yet in all that, it is incredibly useful. Paul says it is truly useful and brings

43

great blessings; but I should not believe that it replaces every-thing else.

What consistently interests people today is the question: Does it give me any advantage?

There one can only, along with Blaise Pascal (d. 1662), rec-ommend the wager. Just live as if it were so, and then you will see whether it brings you any advantage. It is difficult to tell someone that swimming is lovely if he never goes into the water. You have to start sometime. I can describe it: "It is a pleasant feeling when you are being held up by the water, when your muscles can move freely in the water." But you have to do it. And it is just the same with religion. You have to practice it in order to see whether it is useful. I cannot discover, in dry-dock, whether religion helps.

How does it help me, what use is it to me in the whole practical business of coping with everyday life? This confidence in God you were talking about, this knowing where one is going to end up, this knowledge of where life is going, knowing he will take care of me, he is there for me—how does that help me, every day, in my little worries or even my bigger ones? How does faith help me to be better prepared for life's adversities?

Quite concretely, at every moment. It begins with my strug-gling to take some time every day for personal, silent prayer. Meditation, inner prayer, simply being quiet before God, before Christ. My experience—confirmed a hundred times over—is that if I have taken this time early in the morning, then I go into the day in a different way. If I do not man-age that, then I "trudge" or stumble through the day. This orienting of my day to God portends well for the day.

And then I need brief moments now and then, what I call "plongé d'éternité", "little immersions in eternity". If my day is very crowded, as it usually is, with a lot of phone calls, meetings, decisions, and so on, then I sometimes take a short break for a moment to plunge back into God's presence, into eternity, for a couple of seconds, to take a deep breath. I am sure that God forgives me if I look at that, too, from the point of view of its usefulness. It is actively making contact with him with whom I want to be in communication. But as a happy side effect, it helps me through the day.

1.7. Prayer

You have mentioned the importance of taking a short break, of conversation with God—others call it meditation or simply prayer. What is the right way to pray?

There is one rule for that: do it; and a second rule: do not run away. If I have planned to pray for five minutes in silence, then I ought not to run away after four minutes, even if I already have the feeling after three minutes that this time is endlessly long, that I have so much to do, this and that is waiting for me, and much keeps darting through my head that I have to do, ought to be doing, could be doing. This is an old rule, which I heard from a Jesuit priest, though unfortunately I do not always follow it: Keep to the time you have undertaken. The period has to be manageable, but then keep to it. You only learn to pray through praying, just as you only learn to swim through swimming.

Yet there are certain kinds of assistance, techniques, how to float, if I want to learn to swim. It is not any different with praying. Is it a monologue, is it a dialogue, is it talking, is it silence? Is a prayer a request, or is that considered a wrong claim, much too self-centered?

That is all part of it. It is the same as with swimming. Of course, you can learn various styles of swimming, and someone who has gone very far with it can do the butterfly, the crawl, and so on. Most do breaststroke and backstroke, and I think most do much the same in prayer. What is normal prayer? It is a request, and I do not regard it as at all self-centered if I besiege God with my requests. For what does that mean? A prayer of request means that I trust him to be able to do what I cannot. I am asking him, "Help me to make the right decision." Or, "Help this person who cannot at present cope with alcohol, or that sick person." I entrust it to him, and for this reason it is actually a great act of trust and praise of God. I have confidence in him: You can do that. Making requests is actually normal, the breaststroke, if we stay with that image.

The backstroke happens in a more relaxed way. This is meditative prayer, when I am trying to listen, not only within myself, but to God: "What do you have to say to me?"

And yet this is precisely the prayer that withers away completely in everyday life. There, everything is bustle and confusion, noise and haste, never any time, and always stress. Yet the moment we experience pain, sorrow, or need, we immediately call on prayer. Does that count, or is it not pretty shabby, simply shabby human behavior?

I believe that God is infinitely merciful here. "You know of what we are made", it says at one place in the Bible, in

Psalm 103. He knows likewise how negligent we are. I will make a comparison. A mother does not expect her child to say, every day, "Mom, you are so lovely, you are so wonderful, so awesome; I marvel at you, I admire you, I revere you", and so on. She accepts it as a matter of course if the child comes to her, crying, "I've hurt myself", or: "My brother's being nasty to me." That is the way we run crying to God whenever anything hurts us. And perhaps it helps us to remember then that we might actually remember him also from time to time in between. And by the way, I believe that inner gratitude to God is a form of prayer, which—I hope—is very common, perhaps not always consciously, but still present latently, as I find myself every time I come out of here in the direction of Kirchberg and breathe the fresh air, and I am simply thankful that there is such a wonderful place and that I can be there for a couple of hours, a couple of days.

I do think, too, that that is a kind of prayer we ought to practice more often. One experience is quite certain: people who thank God often are happier in their lives.

There are several medical studies being undertaken at present to determine scientifically whether prayer has a measurable effect on health and also to go into the question of whether people who have faith are more likely to be healthy, have a better prognosis. A fascinating question. There are already data that show an effect of prayer on our well-being; it relaxes the body, it can be therapeutic for high blood pressure, heart trouble, and so on. Believers who go to Mass once or twice a week live on average eight years longer than those who stay away from Mass, they say.

Prayer is a marvelous medicine, and there is no doubt it helps. In that respect, it is useful, as the Apostle Paul says.

1.8. How Can God Allow It?

*To what extent is religion a help in coping with life's adversities—
with suffering, pain, sorrow, fear?*

First of all, in that I know that the suffering—even though
at the moment I do not understand it at all—has a meaning
somewhere. Behind it, there is, not a blind fate oppressing
me, but a loving hand. Even if I cannot see it, I know it is
there. We can see this most clearly in profound bereavement.

There is one famous scene in the life of Edith Stein (d.
1942), the great Jewish philosopher who then became a
Christian. In her youth, she had consciously chosen to
become an atheist and had become a student of Edmund
Husserl (d. 1938). There she also came into contact with
Christianity, but she remained a nonbeliever. A young com-
panion and student of Husserl, Adolph Reinach, a brilliant
young philosopher, was killed in 1917 in the First World
War. Edith Stein went to visit his widow. These two gifted
young philosophers had married early. Edith Stein thought
that she would find a broken woman, and yet she met someone who was in deep mourning and at the same time radiant. Looking back to that moment, this meeting at the
Reinachs' home, Edith Stein said, "It was then that I first
understood the power of the Cross."

Later she became a Catholic, entered the Carmelite order,
and was gassed at Auschwitz. Pope John Paul II canonized
her. That experience with the young wife who was not
broken but radiant despite her deep mourning made a great
impression.

*Many people who have that experience of a heavy blow, a serious
illness, or suffering may be able in some sense to understand that.*

Others find it quite cynical to say, in the worst emergency, in a catastrophe, in often measureless suffering, "God is doing this to us, God is speaking to us here." Is it not in fact cynical to say, "Your world is collapsing", and we say, "We can hear God speaking now"?

That is a very important question. Where does God encounter us more, in happiness or in suffering? It is difficult to draw up a balance sheet.

I believe most people would say in suffering—I find that, at any rate.

The writer C. S. Lewis (d. 1963), an Anglican—the *Chronicles of Narnia* are well-known—was convinced that it is in joy. *Surprised by Joy* is the title of his autobiography. And that is how he describes his conversion, and fundamentally the example of Edith Stein is also an experience, not of suffering, but of power within suffering. There was something glowing in this widow that she could not explain: Why was she not completely shattered? I think that experiences of happiness—or perhaps we should be more cautious and say "intensity" or "power"—are probably stronger experiences of God. They stand the test of suffering, but it is not there that they have their roots.

The most profound experience of happiness in my life—I think I can honestly say I have never had a more intense moment of happiness than this—was drinking a cup of hot tea. I was with one of my students—I was a professor at that time—going up the Great Saint Bernard Pass to the Hospice with climbing skins on my skis. I was completely out of shape, and for that stretch, for which a more athletic skiier would take an hour and a quarter, I took a good two and a half hours; and at the end I was so done in that I thought I would never manage the last two hundred yards up to the hospice. Then I came straight into the living room of the hospice of the monks of Saint Bernard—a large guest parlor with an enormous tiled stove that warmed me up. I dropped onto a wooden bench, and a monk with a round, friendly face brought me a big mug of tea. And I was sitting there, drinking this tea, and suddenly I had an indescribable feeling of happiness, such as I have never in my life had so intensely. I do not know why it was. And I did not immediately connect it with God; rather, it was, so to speak, a deep sense that it is good to be alive. An assent to life.

I think such experiences open us to God more than experiences of suffering. Why is it so often experiences of suffering? Because we are so often closed, and suffering often breaks a hole in our wall. Unless an experience of happiness streams in through this breach made by suffering, then we do not have an experience of God. Unless the experience flows in on us, "You are safe, you are being held, I am there"—then suffering is just sheer despair. I have also experienced that.

I am thinking of the situation of a family in which the son tragically died of cancer, and that brought indescribable despair. Suffering in which there was not a ray of light. Then one has to say that this suffering did not lead to any kind of experience of God. The light has to flow in through the crack that suffering has made. Why does it come in for some people, and not for others? That is a great riddle. We have no answer.

And yet this very encounter with despair, with a crisis, with misery—however great or small it may be in my life and whether it is a personal catastrophe or a greater one—that is the touchstone. That is when it happens. It probably has to do with the binding character of faith. Does it stand the test or not? Can I call on something here or not? In my work as a journalist with "Help-TV", I have a great deal to do with people in emergency situations, and my experience has been that in those situations there are two possibilities: some people say, precisely in this situation my faith helped me, or I found it again; it was my consolation, it was my mainstay. Or, the break occurs: it was the proof that there is no God, otherwise that could not have happened to me, could not have happened to those I love. Are both right? Both comprehensible?

You know, from a great deal of experience, better than I do. You cannot and should not lecture people in some serious adversity, in profound suffering and say to them they are "on the wrong track", on the wrong path. You can only try to understand, to be there. One thing is certain, that faith can be a help at such times. Not that the pain cannot be infinitely great on that account. I have seen something just now, with friends—he was forty-three, with six little children, an extraordinarily happy marriage, successful in his career and greatly loved—there was an accident, fishing at sea, he was suddenly snatched away from life. I went straight to them. It was heartbreaking, the pain of the children, his widow, his parents and siblings.

And nonetheless, over it all, in the midst of this sorrow, there was something like a profound and silent consolation. They all had a very deep-rooted faith. And yet the question remains, "Why, why?" That was their first question when I arrived, "Why, why, why, Lord?"

And what is your answer? Whether in this particular situation or in other personal or great catastrophes? Why, God, why do you allow it? The question all people ask, and no answer is ever adequate!

Please, please, no pious empty promises. I believe those who come with those should be chased off without ceremony, as God does in the Book of Job, when Job's three friends talk at length, reproaching him and explaining to him why he is going through this dreadful suffering. In the end, they get a proper slap in the face from God himself, and Job, who struggled with God, argued with him, who went to extremes in his complaint to God, "Why, why, why?", God justifies him. And he punishes the clever theologians, who then have to do penance for their babbling. A fellow Dominican who had bone cancer and suffered really unimaginable pain toward the end—palliative medicine was not so advanced as today—simply said to me, "I ask only one thing of you: In the face of suffering, do not talk so glibly, with pious words. You haven't gone through it." I always have to think of that, whenever such situations arise. I believe the only thing you can do is to be there, to be with the person, weep with them, share their feelings and offer them friendship. And when the opportunity arises, to bring the whole thing before God together, but only when the moment is right.

For sceptics and critics, this has always been proof that there cannot be an almighty, loving God. An almighty, loving God could not allow all that—neither the great tsunami, nor the little personal tsunamis.

If he is a loving God, he would not let us suffer, and if he is almighty, he would not allow these catastrophes to happen. What answer do you have to this question?

Actually, I always feel inclined not to give an answer here. One can put the opposite question, "What kind of consolation would it be to say that he does not exist? What would you get from that?" I can only say, I cannot explain it to you, I can simply tell you one thing: the God in whom I believe did not pass suffering by in Jesus, his Son. He did not explain it away, did not say, as some religions or philosophies do, "That is only deception, illusion; forget it." He wept with those who were weeping; he did not look away. He did not kill; rather, he let himself be killed; he did not judge; rather, he allowed himself to be judged. I can hold this God before your eyes and then see whether this God has an answer for you, too.

Are these situations, however, in which you, you who are on the way to being a Christian, becoming a Christian, could argue with this God or even get angry with him?

There are moments like that. I have to say that in my personal life, I have so far been spared any really great suffering. I have experienced a great deal of suffering around me; I have seen suffering in my own family, even human disasters, but never anything like what I saw in the tsunami in Banda Aceh, in Indonesia, with my own family completely killed by the disaster and only me surviving. I have not experienced Auschwitz or the Communist prisons. In my life, without my deserving it, things have gone well on the whole. I have had many loving people around me. I grew up in relative security, in spite of some difficulties. That is why I am particularly reticent when faced with great suffering, because I have not experienced it in my own body, my own flesh.

What did shake me was the situation I found after the tsunami, when people could not be reached with comfort.

That does happen. Then you stand helpless before it—a radical hopelessness. How can such people be reached? You can only give them attention. But when faith is entirely absent, then it is very, very difficult.

But that means, in the end, that there are questions to which God does not give you an answer?

Yes. To which he will perhaps some day give me an answer, but to which I have no answer now. There is one great question that has much preoccupied me during the past year, and that is the question of cruelty in nature. When you see the praying mantis and watch how the female devours the male during mating, you wonder why there are these unspeakable horrors in nature. There are countless examples. Is this only our human imagination? Does the praying mantis, or the male that is devoured while he mates with her, feel pain? The female does not do that out of wickedness, but because she is programmed to do it. Yet what kind of a programmer is this? I have serious questions about this, and the questions are also often put to me when people say, "Where is an 'intelligent design' in creation, then, if there are such horrors?" I have to admit that I have no ready-made answer to that. I know just one thing, that this world is in transit and that for as long as it is in transit, there will be sighing and groaning and death in it. Why that is so, why God did not create a world in which there is no suffering? I do not know. Could he have created that? Could he have created a world in which we are completely free of suffering? As we are created now, with our freedom, we men make a lot of blunders and cause a lot of suffering; and as nature, into which we are placed, is created now, there are a great many appalling things, despite all the marvelous beauty of nature. As to why it is so, I have no final answer to that, but it is certainly one of the first questions I shall ask him, when I am able to question him face to face.

1.9. Believing—But How?

How much does a religion require of me? How much effort does it take to believe?

Karl Barth (d. 1968), the great twentieth-century Protestant theologian, said in the days of his youth that religion is idolatry. That sounds very radical. What did he mean by that? He meant that when religion is one sphere of life, a hollow, gilded, Sunday sphere wrapped in tinsel, then it becomes idolatry. Then people make something sweet out of religion for amusement on Sundays or an opportunity for "Sunday finery".

One may rightly contrast with that what "believing" means in the Bible. Believing, at its most profound, means total sacrifice. Thomas Aquinas (d. 1274) defines religion as "totum se deo vovere", "dedicating", "sacrificing", or "surrendering oneself completely to God". Then the question naturally arises, "Can that be done?" "Is that livable?" I cannot crawl about on my knees from dawn till dark. I cannot pray the whole day. What does it mean, that religion imposes a total claim on a man, so to speak, and is no longer limited to a little sphere on Sunday? Religion is the fundamental axis on which life turns, the primal link between man and God. And if you understand religion that way, then religion turns out to be something constitutive for man. If I start from the assumption that man has been created by

God, then this fundamental relationship with God is, so to speak, the pivotal point in life, the umbilical cord linking us to the origin and goal.

Yet this umbilical cord, or this contact with life, does not need to be and cannot be permanently activated. In this respect, religion is one subportion of my life. I cannot have Sunday all day. I cannot have Sunday all week. I cannot pray all day. I also have to work. I have to sleep. I spend time with other people, and so on. The question is only: Is religion something like the basic melody of my life. Is it the existential, the fundamental determination of my life? Is it a kind of horizon within which everything in my life happens, whether consciously or unconsciously? One thing we can certainly say: Religion cannot be just a small sphere to which I give my attention for an hour on Sundays, and, apart from that, I behave as if there were no God. That is what Karl Barth was fighting against when he said that religion is idolatry.

But is it hard work, in the sense of being demanding, of there being a constant challenge and of being plagued by doubts? So that even for a cardinal, it remains in that sense hard work and a challenge?

It absolutely remains a challenge, because man is forgetful. In the Bible, especially in the Old Testament, there is a basic saying that is always appearing: "Do not forget! Remember!" It says in the Old Testament, very sensibly and with a great knowledge of human nature, "Then, when you are in the Promised Land, after the trials of the wilderness, forty years in the desert, after all the fears of the exodus from Egypt and all the testing you have undergone and all the suffering you have gone through; when you sit well-fed under your fig tree and the land is there for you to enjoy and things go well with you, then do not forget!" And that is why biblical religion is a religion of remembering. Bring to mind that you came up out of Egypt, that you were a slave and you have been freed. Do not forget your God. That is hard work.

But if we may come back again to the comparison with education. Parents, too, must constantly remind their children, "Stand up straight!" Many little reminders go to make up an education. In that sense, religion is hard work. Because it is working against gravity, against what is comfortable, and it makes demands. In the evening, I am tired and I go to bed. Kneeling down again for evening prayer, that is difficult: "Oh, I'll just lie down tonight, and tomorrow ..." These constant little victories over myself, so that I do not just go my own way, are what make religion a living thing. The other side of the coin is that when I have trained myself, so to say, in religion, when I consistently make a regular practice of going to Sunday Mass, praying, and so forth, then this has a positive effect: religion becomes a home, it supports me, comforts me, helps and encourages me. But that only happens if I practice it.

That is why they used to say that religion is a virtue. In the classical doctrine on virtues, religion has been a part of justice since Plato, one of the cardinal virtues along with prudence, temperance, and fortitude. Justice, is what we owe one another. Justice toward God is what we owe to God. We owe God thanks, attention, recognition—religion. A religious person is someone who dutifully expresses his gratitude to God—I am deliberately framing this somewhat provocatively. In this regard, religion is a virtue. If I practice it regularly, it becomes a good habit. I find it much easier than I would if I only practiced it during all the holy seasons. And it even becomes something enjoyable and lovely.

Does it make people happier?

Without a doubt. It is easier to live and easier to die.

Does it make me a better person?

Every virtue makes me better. If I have practiced the virtue of patience, then I am certainly better than if I had not practiced it and were impatient. If I have practiced the virtue of prudence, through a great deal of exercise, trouble, and effort, and the advice of wise and experienced people, then that makes me better that if I were imprudent. If I have the virtue of temperance, I will certainly be better. Aristotle, the father of the Western doctrine on virtue, said, "Virtue is what makes a person better. Vice is what makes a person troublesome."

But that would mean that religion is a path to human integrity?

Absolutely.

How is faith proof against crises, or how is it subject to crises? Have you always known that your path was the right one?

I certainly think I can say that I have never doubted that the gospel is truly the way. I have never found anywhere else a better, clearer, more human way than the gospel. There is no doubt that Jesus' way is not a simple one, and yet the feeling has never left me that this is the right way. I only have doubts concerning myself. Where have I left this path?

When did I lose sight of it, and how shall I find it again if I have lost it or if it is not clear to me? What does it mean now, in this concrete situation, to follow the path of Jesus? That is where there are doubts.

Does even a cardinal do wrong?

He would not otherwise need to go to confession.

I do not know—does he go to confession, then?

Of course he goes to confession; even regularly, almost every week. That is essential, because that is our opportunity to sharpen our conscience, to give some attention to subtleties and not be too coarse in the view we take of a situation, or of our own life.

It is always said: in confession, people tell their troubles and among the regulars at the bar they tell their sins. Is there in your own experience or in your practice as a confessor a "principal sin" among us human beings?

I would first say that hearing confessions, the ministry of the confessional, the sacrament of penance is for me, as a priest, actually the most beautiful. I then feel with certitude, "Now I really know why I became a priest." Why? Not because the confessions are so interesting. Basically, you have to say that sins are always banal. There is no originality in sin. Only what is good is original. The good is exciting, beautiful, and alive. Sin is always stupid, banal, and very unoriginal, dreadfully repetitive. And that is why it is so moving to meet with people's honesty, their wretchedness, and often their greatness.

It is true, what you say, that people often talk about their problems in the confessional. In the majority of cases, it is this way: first comes a certain catalogue of sins. If, for instance, someone says, "I have been angry", then I respond with the question, "Are you under a great deal of stress?" and then all the worries, the troubles, and the burdens come out. If I say, "How can you bear all that?" then I hear a testimony of faith that really shakes me, from people who are bearing incredible things and not resigned to it.

Drawing strength from confession is an aspect of the sacrament of penance that is far too little perceived. Confession is first of all an admission of sins. But in the absolution, strength is indeed imparted. The sacrament of penance is at least as much the imparting of strength as it is the forgiveness of sins. For me, going to confession means laying my failings before God, in front of a qualified witness, since saying them out loud is important. Putting it into words is also so important psychologically. But what is most important for me in confession is drawing strength from it. It is a weekly or regular power station.

But that also means that this is a situation where we see if a priest is a good psychologist?

Yes, although for me it is not decisive whether he is a good psychologist here; rather, he should be primarily a "channel" for divine forgiveness. Naturally, the advice he gives, what he says to someone, even the questions he asks, may be very helpful. It is above all important that I carry out this act, saying clearly in front of someone what is not in order in my life, and know that he is truly and effectively granting me the mercy of Jesus. For me personally—and I recommend this to anyone who wants to follow a personal path of faith—it is important to have a regular confessor. Like the family doctor, who knows you. Then you do not always need to go through the entire case history. Then the additional, clarifying words can be very important. And that does not need to be much.

Does God really forgive everything?

Absolutely. He forgives everything. I need only have the faintest beginnings of contrition. But without the element of contrition, God's mercy has nothing it can take hold of.

Now, we are living at present in an age in which we only pay attention to something if it is causing problems. Only when we lose something do we realize its value. When we are ill, we can measure the importance of good health. Only when a relationship breaks up, when the partner has gone, do we know that we have occasionally invested too little in it. Is the same true of faith, of religion?

Religion can hardly be learned in an intensive crash course, because it, like every virtue, needs to be practiced. We know that from all the other areas. It is just as with sports: if I start to think, after my first heart attack, that it would actually be good for me to be a little active, I would not become athletic right off the bat. Everything needs to be cultivated, that is clear, and faith has to be cultivated just like a plant, it has to be cultivated like a relationship. The reason our relationship with God is so discreet and so easily forgotten is that God is a very discreet partner. When you live in a relationship, then there is someone opposite you, and that is demanding, it is there, and then you notice—sometimes, unfortunately, too late—that you have neglected the relationship. God is so quiet that we can live for a long time without noticing that this relationship is withering away. I do not believe that it can die off completely. It may be so neglected on our side that it is practically dead, but God does not abandon us. He brings back memories of himself and gives us signs.

Yet spiritual experience in the writings of the great masters of the Christian life, and basically in a similar way in other religions, tells us that it is not for nothing that we have to practice. In Latin, to practice is *exercere*, and that is where the English word "exercise" comes from. Spiritual exercises are enjoined on priests and members of religious orders. Once a year, they should take a week out for that. The basis for this is the experience that you have to practice the spiritual life. Regularity is the beginning and end of all exercise, whether bodily, mental, or spiritual.

1.10. The Final Way

Why does dying give us such problems?

Because it is against nature.

Is it?

And at the same time entirely natural. Everything that comes into being passes away. We indeed also come into being, we are conceived and born, but we are created, not to pass away, but for eternal life. Somehow death is always a scandal. I find that I am simply unable to imagine that a person is dead. I cannot imagine it. As when Cardinal König died—who, heaven knows, was elderly, ninety-eight years old—I was unable to imagine that he was simply gone. There is something correct about that, because the dead are not simply gone. We do not sink into nothingness.

We have so great a fear of it.

At the same time, death is sometimes a release. People even say, "It is a good thing he was able to die", when someone was very ill. "It was a release." That is of course also true, yet actually death is contrary to nature. In the Bible, in the Book of Wisdom, it says, "God did not make death; but through the devil's envy death entered the world."

You said before that religion, faith, has to be practiced. You cannot learn it quickly when things get tight? Can one start to believe on one's deathbed? Have you ever had this experience, that something happened then to people—at the end?

I have experienced that, very movingly, with my father. That certainly happens. I am only afraid that we also have to learn how to die. Formerly—from 1550 to about 1780— there was a special literary genre, the art of dying, the *Ars moriendi*. In the library of our religious house, I grouped together the books I found about this. It became a whole little library. Then, with the Enlightenment, that stopped. How do you learn how to die? There used to be special manuals for that. People prepared themselves for it, they got ready for it. They knew that this hour was surely coming, and they did not want to sneak away from life. People felt that sudden death was something bad. Today we say, "That was a merciful death", if someone simply drops dead and is gone. Formerly they prayed explicitly, "ab improvisa morte libera nos, Domine!"—"From unforeseen death, deliver us, O Lord!"—because people did not wish to take this most important step in life unconsciously. People prepared themselves.

If you look at the old prayers for the dying, the Church's old ritual contains an unbelievably fascinating "psychology of dying". The dying person was accompanied with a kind of worship service, first with prayers that the dying person himself spoke aloud as long as he could, and then prayers said on the dying person's behalf. At the moment of the *transitus*, the passing on, there is an ancient prayer that probably goes back even to early Jewish tradition: "Profiscere anima christiana"—"Go forth, O Christian soul." I find that fascinating. The dying person was urged to jump off, so to speak: Go now! "Go forth, O Christian soul!" Set out on your journey! It is now time to let go. Go on your way. And then it is marvelously beautiful, how it says in this long and ancient prayer, "May Christ show you the graciousness of his countenance. May angels come to meet you. May Mary welcome you." A series of saints are then named. "May your place be in Paradise today." That is a reference to the righteous criminal, to whom Jesus promised, "Today you will be with me in Paradise." May you find rest in the *amoena virentia*, the lovely verdant meadows of Paradise. It is with this prayer, at the moment of death, that the dying person is sent on over, so to speak.

And then there was a tradition, which I was still able to experience myself in the monastery, of not leaving the body alone before the burial. A wake was kept. Today it is removed and put in a freezer somewhere. Until not so very long ago, people used to keep vigil by the body, to pray beside it. Behind that there is an ancient knowledge of mankind, which is also to be found in the Tibetan book of the dead, in the Egyptian book of the dead, everywhere in the old traditions of mankind, that the soul must be accompanied on its way over. The Greek myth of Charon, who ferries souls over the river, the testing of souls, weighing souls in the balance—all these images are addressing a human awareness that souls need to be accompanied on their way "over to the other side". That is why the dead person was not left alone until the burial, that watch was kept beside them and company provided on their way. We have simply lost a great part of human culture in relation to dying.

I have read that in former East Germany, thus in the new provinces of the Federal Republic, up to 40 percent of people who die are no longer buried. The bodies are disposed of like hazardous waste. So much of our knowledge about life, and thus also about dying, has been lost, and that is why we feel so helpless in the face of death. And we no longer have any rituals. We do not know how to deal with dying. Formerly everyone knew the prayers for the dying by heart. I can recall a student from Lötschental in the Upper Valais, who wrote a dissertation that I supervised. In the mountain valley from which he comes the old traditions have survived a very long time. He told how his parents and his other relatives of the older generation knew all the prayers for the dying by heart. These were long prayers, with a ritual that went with them. Those people knew how to deal with death. We are helpless in the face of death. We use machines, excessively, to keep people on life support, and then when it is all over, the body is disposed of.

Thank God, that is changing a bit. A little while ago, on the Baumgarten Heights, in one of the wards of that hospital, I blessed a death room that the doctors and nurses have had arranged there, so that the dying and the dead are in a dignified setting, where their relatives can take leave of them. It seems to me very good and important, that traditions like those are being continued again.

Chapter 2

Faith and the World

2.1. Church and Politics

In magazines all over the world, at present, there are articles about a return to religion. Jesus on the cover, and Pope Benedict XVI likewise. What suggests to you that religion is making a comeback? Why is there a growing desire to have answers to the fundamental questions of life?

There are probably many reasons for it. I think one reason is that so-called secularization—that is, the disappearance of religion from public life, which has been strongly characteristic of the past fifty or a hundred years—leaves people feeling very disconsolate. The consumer market, which I do not regard as altogether bad, fulfills only the most superficial needs. These needs are inescapable and important, but this does not satisfy the spirit. And the more we are able to have everything, the more we notice that we do not have those things you cannot buy. That is probably the reason why the longing for religion has not died out.

There is a second phenomenon, which is bothering political scientists terribly at the moment, and all over the world there are symposiums being held about it: the resurgence of religion as a factor in global politics. It had been believed that religion could be excluded and political questions could be solved with diplomacy, economics, and military intervention. More recently it has been discovered—and whether we like it or not, it is a fact—that religions are everywhere becoming a political factor once more, in a very substantial way: a certain kind of Christian witness in the politics of the United States, the strongly increased political influence of Islam as a factor in global politics, Hinduism in India, or Buddhism in Sri Lanka, to name but a few examples. Politicians and political scientists are saying nowadays, "We have to take the religious factor into account more seriously in the political debate and in politics itself. We made a mistake in simply forgetting that."

How do you assess that? That is after all a discussion we cannot hold without some degree of concern, since we see it as a great achievement, having made this very strict separation between Church and state.

I am first noticing it now as a fact myself . . .

As a fact, a development, that has to be regarded with great concern?

Yes. One that will certainly be very much in the forefront of our minds in the next few years. Right now, I can say, only from the Christian point of view, that I think that the two-thousand-year history of Christianity's experience with politics is very instructive and could also serve as a model for others. For in the course of those two thousand years, we have gone through not a few failures in the history of the relations between religion and politics. We therefore ought to be more cautious in our judgments about other religions, when we demand of others the state we have reached in Christianity today, without reflecting that our own history is very complex and filled with conflict. What is marvelous in the Christian vision of the relations between Church, religion, and politics? And what has Christianity learned in the course of the centuries? Through very painful experience?

What is fundamental is something Jesus once said casually when a snare was set for him relating to the obligation to pay taxes to the occupying power that was depriving Israel of freedom at the time. Is it permissible to pay taxes to Caesar? Jesus had them show him a coin, on which was the emperor's image. He asked, "Whose image is this?"— "Caesar's."—"Well then, give to Caesar what belongs to Caesar, and give to God what belongs to God." At first sight, this reply appears to be like a dodge to get out of a trick question. If he had said, "It is permissible to pay taxes", then people would have said, "He is a collaborator, on the side of the occupying power, and not a truly pious Jew." If he had said, "It is not permissible to pay taxes to Caesar", then people would have said, "He is a rebel", and could have reported him to the Romans. He saw through that, of course, and reproached them for their hypocrisy. He took Caesar's coin, with Caesar's image on it, implying, "You do business with this money, why put trick questions to me? You agree to the compromises that are necessary in life."

Yet beyond that, on a deeper level, is a view that became historically powerful and profoundly influences our present understanding of religion and politics. That is the clear distinction, not a separation, but a distinction between the profane and the spiritual, between religion and politics.

You said that for a long time we have excluded the religious element from political life, and that is now catching up with us. If we look at other world religions and their close links with political systems, the examples are numerous, worldwide, and disquieting. And, above all, what about this separation? How much politics can a religion stand?

You cannot separate them, but you absolutely must distinguish between them. The Second Vatican Council, in its Pastoral Constitution on the Church in the Modern World, quite clearly emphasizes this important distinction yet again. It speaks there of the relative autonomy of particular spheres. What is meant by that?

We do not expect the economy to be managed according to religious criteria but in accordance with good economic criteria. Among those good economic criteria are ethics, whether the ethics of economics or ethics per se. And fundamental religious values and attitudes are a part of good ethics. Yet a bishop does not understand anything about economics simply because he is the pastor of a religious community, a community of faith, and he should therefore not to be taking part in economic decisions. He should indicate the fundamental principles, the ethical standards, but not be managing the economy.

The same is true of all the various branches of knowledge. It is not a good thing when religion dictates how science should go about its business, how it should conduct its research. It is important that there be an ethics of science, above all, an ethics for the scientist. Yet that is none other than the ethics every person should follow, laid down in the Ten Commandments. But there is of course something like a dialogue between religion and science, in which certain orientations, from the faith, certain boundaries have at least to be addressed. But it is not a good thing if the science of a given faith community is being decided by those responsible for its religion.

The same, of course, holds good for politics. One example, of which I have had direct experience and also in discussions, is Iran. There, above the political leadership, there is a second, supreme stratum, the religious. And in very many spheres, the final decisions lie with the religious leadership, not with the political leaders. That has fatal consequences. Every mistake in economics is blamed on the religious leaders. If the Iranian airline is in difficulties, what business do the religious authorities have getting involved there?

In Christian civilization this separation is fundamental, as we have said, and was implemented by Jesus himself. We know from history that in practice, this distinction has been achieved only with great effort. For the first three centuries it was quite clear; Christianity was not a state religion anywhere at all; rather, it was persecuted. But when it became a state religion in the Roman Empire, and in other countries like Ethiopia and Armenia, a new situation arose. The emperor had become a Christian. The laws of the empire were decided by a Christian emperor, by a Christian state religion, and the ecclesiastical hierarchy inevitably acquired a new and enormous influence on the whole life of society. We know from history that with this began a struggle between the *imperium* and the *sacerdotium*, between emperor and pope, between ecclesiastical and secular powers that lasted for centuries. We will not trace that history here. It lasted at least from 315 into the twentieth century; and then, with difficult labor pains, led to what the Second Vatican Council then solemnly laid down as Church doctrine and expressed as henceforth determinative for the Catholic Church.

So today, priests, bishops, and members of the hierarchy are basically not allowed to hold any political office, and most certainly not a military one. They were not allowed to do so in the centuries of the Constantinian era, so that practically ever since early times bishops and priests were never allowed to take part in military actions. A great many of them, however, were active in politics as sovereigns. The pope had his own state, the Papal States, up to 1870, and up to the end of the Papal States he was head of state, with his own army and with his own national sovereignty. Nowadays we simply cannot imagine that. The little Vatican State is, if anything, a symbol, even if it is sovereign. Today, quite rightly, we see that the Church does not need her own state in order to exist. Up to the end of the Holy Roman Empire of the German nation, the bishops were in many cases sovereign princes, so that they held secular power within their spiritual principalities. We may think of the archbishop of Salzburg and many others.

All that is history for us. It is certainly not yet history in Islam. Will it ever become history for them? Will so clear a distinction ever be made between religion and politics as it is among us? Let us hope so.

Is that not precisely one of the decisive points in the controversy between Christianity and Islam, along with all the circumstances that follow today from the fact that here a religion is encountering a political system, and we are always mixing this circumstance into the discussions?

Yes, that is certainly one of the basic difficulties. We can only bear witness, and do so even in discussions with Muslims, that Christianity has suffered no disadvantages—that, on the contrary, it has been good for Christianity that the clear distinction between spiritual and secular things is no longer disputed, a distinction that Jesus intended and that for so long was not fully applied. We can only wish that this will come to Islam. It is good for a religious authority when it does not attempt to be a secular authority. Yet this distinction presupposes something that is perhaps not familiar to Islam in its religion.

For Christianity, man is a citizen of two states; he is a citizen of the divine state, the city of God, the Church, the heavenly Jerusalem, and he is a citizen of his state here on earth. Yet he never merges completely into being a citizen of his country. In the Christian view of man, man is always more than merely the citizen of a country. He is also a citizen of the heavenly Jerusalem. He has, as it were, the rights of a citizen, as Paul puts it, "en tois uranois", "in the heavens", because Christ has made us members of the kingdom of God, even though we are still on our way there.

This dual citizenship, this belonging in two places, has always made dictators absolutely furious, because they want people to belong to them entirely. Hitler wanted only one salvation, that is, his own—"Heil Hitler". And he could not bear the thought that salvation should come from anybody but Hitler. That is why he cultivated a pseudo-religion around his power and persecuted not only Jews to death, but also Christians. Every dictatorship has, up to now, tried to get people entirely under control and has failed at that particularly with Christianity, because it grants people a transcendental, heavenly citizenship as well and thus always withdraws them a little from the secular authority.

And yet it is not entirely easy to understand. On the one hand, you are saying, we find ourselves in trouble at present because we do not live out and incorporate religious values in politics. On the other hand, you emphasize how important it is, to draw this line separating politics and religion. So what now? Isn't this a little bit like, "Wash me, but don't make me wet"?

Our situation here in Austria is perhaps particularly instructive. Up to 1918, Catholics and the Catholic Church lived under the protection of the emperor. Catholicism, as the religion of the ruling dynasty, was the privileged religion, even though the religious tolerance of the Habsburg Monarchy remains a magnificent example, whose standards regarding religious tolerance have unfortunately yet to be reached in many places. But the emperor was the "apostolic majesty". He appointed the bishops. Rome merely confirmed them. It was a state church. When in the year 1918/1919, this closeness between altar and throne was suddenly relinquished, that was an incredible break, as indeed the end of the monarchy was generally for many people a much more severe break.

The period between the wars was characterized by what has been called "political Catholicism". Cardinal Theodore Innitzer was Minister for Social Affairs, and Monsignor Ignaz Seipel was Federal Chancellor. The "prelate without mercy", he was called. That shows that this intermediate phase, following the end of state religion, was still a very difficult time of seeking. In addition, there was the deep rift between "reds" and "blacks" in the period between the wars, which then—because it was not repaired in time—contributed to the drama of the brownshirts.

After the war, something started to happen that had a great influence on the situation in Austria. The so-called "Mariazell Manifesto" of 1952, from the Katholikentag [an annual cultural gathering for German Catholics], although it never actually existed at all in this form, has gone down in history as this:

"A free Church in a free state"—that was a new phase, and we may thank Cardinal König for having finally brought this about. The Church is not linked to any political party.

She has members in all the political parties. That is why she consciously avoids associating herself with party politics. The parties themselves decide how close they are going to be to the Church, through their programs. She might be close to one party on one point, and on another point closer to another party. That is how the Church has lived in Austria in recent decades. That has of course led to too great a withdrawal from politics on the Church side—this was, so to speak, the swing of the pendulum in the other direction— rightly withdrawing from party politics, but wrongly from the politics of society. In recent years there have repeatedly been clear signs that a stronger involvement of the Church in the political life of society is felt desirable even by some politicians and is being lived by Catholics. I see that as a positive development.

I will mention one example where this has become very clear: the Austrian constitutional convention. In that instance, not only Catholics, but all the recognized Christian churches succeeded in joining together to work out a common position for this constitutional convention. And we reported this shared position at the hearing in parliament. It was something of a surprise for the political parties in our country to find all the Christians speaking with a common voice, unequivocally taking up an independent position vis-à-vis the political parties, in talks with everyone, exchanging ideas, and yet formulating a clear position of their own. As a result of this, in the documentation of the constitutional convention the position of the Austrian Volkspartei, that of the Social Democrats and that of the so-called "ökumenischen Experten gruppe" (group of ecumenical experts) were each listed separately, so that it became clear that the Christians are intensively involved in discussions about social policy and have a quite open and straightforward relationship with the parties, but they are not simply identical with one or more parties.

If we think of the discussion about the European constitution, it concerned this very question.

We were successful with the European constitution, insofar as one can talk about being "successful" in that case . . .

Nothing has succeeded so far.

. . . it succeeded insofar as, as a result of German and Austrian practice, the subject of religion occurs in the constitution at all. Unfortunately, not in the preamble, we were unsuccessful there, and that remains a very sore point; yet in the end, article 52 is a remarkable text with regard to the situation of the churches and religious denominations in society in the European Union.

Yet why does it remain "a very sore point", if, on the other hand, you emphasize that the distinction between religion and politics is so important? Why should religion be in the preamble?

That is perhaps precisely the crucial point. What does the presence of religion in politics mean? There is the position of those who say that the state needs a supradenominational, general "civil religion". We say there is no such thing. There are only concrete religions. We are therefore sceptical and negative about the proposal that we agree on some kind of "civil religion", which should constitute the general religious horizon of the political.

But we do believe that the denominational churches and religions, each with its own identity, are an important element in civil society, too. It should at least be demanded of civil society that it does not regard the factor of religion as something objectionable or even damaging. On this point, Jürgen Habermass, in his conversation with Joseph Cardinal Ratzinger, said something interesting, I believe, even groundbreaking. Democracy must be capable of religion, compatible with religion. It would be a bad sign for a democracy if it had no place for denominations, religions.

What is the significance of denominations? I believe our Austrian constitutional convention showed that very well. Religions are an important element in civil society in many spheres: in the social and educational spheres, in the transmission of values, in forming life styles, and also, as they say in philosophical terms, in contingency management: to cope with pain and death. Society necessarily has to deal with these things, yet it cannot answer them from its own resources. It needs help with that. Civil society as such offers no model for contingency management or coping with death. Religions contribute that to civil society, and that is something which requires, on the other hand, that politics factor religion in as a relevant element.

I think we have a good example of this in Austria. The debate on euthanasia is a classic case for the question, "How do we deal with old age, pain, disability, and death, in civil society?" How do we deal with dying, and with contingency? We have been successful in Austria, and this is certainly due above all to the Christian Churches, in shaping a political consensus and in deliberately making it beyond dispute that euthanasia is not a question in Austria. There are other means available to deal with that: terminal care, the hospice movement, palliative medicine, and so on. This, I believe, is a very successful example of the way religion and civil society can reinforce one another. Within the framework of a liberalizing concept of society, one might say, "Why are religions interfering here? It is the business of politics to decide whether euthanasia is to be authorized or not." This concept of society tends toward totalitarianism. Pope Benedict XVI has called that "the dictatorship of relativism". Christians, too, are citizens of the state, and when they introduce their view of man into social discourse, they are doing something not only legitimate, but even necessary. That is why it would at least be tending toward totalitarian if one were to say that religious motives may not be incorporated into politics. Of course they may. Those are the convictions of the citizens.

Should the Church speak out more clearly and more often in politics?

Who is the Church?

You, for example, as an important representative of the Church, a cardinal and archbishop.

I am a part of the Church. As bishop, I am a pastor—the chief pastor is Christ—I am pastor of the Catholic Church in the archdiocese of Vienna. Whenever I speak out, that is one voice of the Church, but it is certainly not the only one. One time, an official from Brussels was with me—an Austrian who works in Brussels, a Catholic who is active in a parish—and he said that it is a pity that the Church has so little presence in Brussels. I said, "How is that, since you are there?" And he looked at me, somewhat dumbfounded. I said, "Well now, you are after all a practicing Catholic. You are an official in Brussels, so the Church is present there."

The Church has to speak out—yes, but where? The factory manager who is a Catholic, the official who is Catholic, the hairdresser who is Catholic and stands by her faith, and my nice pedicurist, Poldi. Everyone in the business knows she is a Catholic, she stands by it, and even talks about her faith with her customers. "Go on," she says, "you pray a bit more, and then it will be better for you." That is what I call the presence of the Church. Each and every person ... we are all Church.

What do I expect of the Church in politics? My expectation is that someone like Alfred Gusenbauer, who used to serve Mass, whose mother sings in the church choir, who says he is a Catholic—and I believe him—will translate Christian principles into his politics. And we expect the same thing, quite rightly, from someone like Wilhelm Molterer, who is a Catholic, who publicly acknowledges belonging to the Church and is a committed Christian. I believe both of them are trying to do this. The emphasis will perhaps be different, because as a Christian you can be more to the "right" or to the "left", can lay more stress on the economic aspects or on the social aspects; but those people who publicly confess their faith are the Church, wherever they are.

But how do you decide whether or not to speak out on some political question? Is it not precisely in social questions that a clear profile is demanded of the Church? You can read in the Bible that the Church is on the side of the weakest. Does that not need to be said much more clearly today?

I always recall that the Church is a choir with many voices, not always very harmonious, and sometimes the voices are somewhat dissonant because there are so many different ones. That is why, on many questions, I do not speak out, because I am convinced that in this case, for example, Caritas is quite clearly representing the Church's position. Caritas is an essential element of the Church. The Church has three basic forms, three fundamental dimensions: proclamation of the Word of God, celebration of the liturgy, and service to neighbors. That is why Caritas is an essential element of the Church. Although it happens, from time to time, that I am not entirely in agreement with the director of Caritas in Vienna, Michael Landau, in his assessment of a situation or in his comments, actually I almost always have to say, "Yes, that is exactly the position of the Church", and I am thankful that he represents it competently and very, very convincingly, also quite controversially, so that there is disagreement, but that need not surprise us.

Does it not look, then, as if you are sometimes hiding behind Caritas?

No, I do not need to hide behind it, because Caritas is the voice of the Church. It is, perhaps, not clearly enough appreciated when we say "Caritas" and "the Church". I always say, then, that the Church is Caritas, and Caritas is the Church. There are also of course other emphases; in a conversation with the economy, or with industry, for example, the emphases are not always quite the same as that of Caritas. I experienced that again the other day in a conversation with the Industrialists' Association. Then I remind people that Caritas has to be one-sided, in a certain sense. It is trying to be a voice for those who have no political lobby. Business, industry, commerce—all these large groups have powerful and effective lobbies. Do the homeless, single mothers, or pensioners, at the bottom of the financial scale, have a lobby?

Caritas, in cooperation with others, has built up a marvelous lobby for hospice work. It therefore has to speak with a certain loudness, and I wholeheartedly support that, because this part of society must have a voice. And since Caritas is an organization large enough to have a voice, it has to raise this voice, too. When Caritas has spoken out on some subject, I regard it as unnecessary to duplicate that. When Caritas is heavily criticized, then I back them up and say, "That is our voice."

But Caritas supports social institutions, like other charitable institutions. When you say that Caritas is the Church, that is not entirely true in practice. Caritas is not paid for 100 percent by the Church, for example; she pays only a very small percentage. So Caritas is not the Church.

You cannot say that, since even Catholic private schools are thus subsidized by the state in that the teaching staff are paid by the state. This is our Austrian model of cooperation. We should remember that this takes a great burden off the state. For in both the school system and in the charitable domain, the, so to speak, outsourcing of services by the state to private organizations is financially very much better for the state, because in fact the Church also makes a substantial contribution of her own. I cannot specify any percentage for you, but in the area of schools the whole administrative and building expense goes to the owners of the school, that is, the Church. That saves the state many, many millions every year. And it is much the same with the charitable institutions. The state or the Länder [regional states] have good reason to cooperate with Caritas or other private social institutions, non-state social institutions, because this outsourcing means great savings for the state. So that is not a kindness that the state grants to Caritas or denominational schools; rather, it is a service that the state, so to speak, purchases from private contractors, a cooperative action that is quite advantageous for the state as well. A third example would be the Church hospitals, which cost considerably less than public hospitals.

Nevertheless, it sounds as if you are saying, "For the great social questions, on the whole we have Caritas . . ." And yet these are the most urgent political questions at the present time: unemployment, the shortage of nursing staff, the increase in poverty worldwide, the situation of the disabled, political asylum, and much more. Would these things not be the argument for the Church? To say, that is our USP (unique selling point), we have the social skills— that is not clearly evident to people today.

A quite personal reply here: I always hesitate to take a position publicly myself. I often speak out, but I do so deliberately—with my weekly commentaries on the Gospel readings, for instance—in the area of preaching. For the first task is proclaiming the good news. Why? Because the good news offers the motivation for charitable action, for practicing love of one's neighbor. If this is not put into practice, as Caritas is trying to do, in a, so to speak, concrete, visible, tangible form, then the Church would be lacking an essential element.

Preaching, however, always also offers the horizon of worship for this. Jesus talked about love of God and love of one's neighbor in the same breath. The first commandment is: You shall love God with all your heart and with all your strength. And the second is like it: You shall love your neighbor as yourself. Preaching and the ministry of our Caritas are inseparable. I see the task of a bishop as being primarily to keep the word of God alive in a society, to keep worship present for people, and to hope that out of this will spring as deep a motivation as possible for loving God and one's neighbor. I see a certain danger if I were constantly to comment on questions on which Michael Landau, Franz Küberl, or other colleagues in Caritas are speaking out with the greatest competence and commitment. I believe my task is—in season or out of season, as Paul says—to preach the gospel.

One political question on which you have made a clear statement concerns the discussion about shopping hours, which is ultimately a question of symbolic significance for many discussions between economic interests, profit, on the one hand, and human well-being, on the other. There are many economic reasons in favor. You, like some leading politicians, are clearly against. Do you think the discussion is over, or is it going to come up again and again?

The discussion about Sunday opening is not over, but we will fight on quite decidedly and energetically, and I sense, and can see and read, that the number of people fighting with us is growing. More and more people are saying that Sunday ought not to be given up. This last island of freedom should not be sacrificed to the almighty idol of mammon. For even the ancient Jewish tradition was aware, and still is aware, that the Sabbath—or Sunday for us—is a day of freedom. That is the day, in the rhythm of the week, when a man experiences that he is not just a hamster running in a wheel, a slave to work, but he is a free person.

There are posters from the Federal Economic Chamber with the slogan, "If the economy does well, we all do well." Is that so?

It is right up to a certain point. If the economy is doing well, then the material basis of existence is secure, and that is something positive. You only have to look here at countries in which the material basis of existence is badly managed or is inadequate—and there are many countries in the world where that is so. There is no doubt that is a difficult situation for people, and it is then that much more difficult to live a decent human life. Yet in spite of everything, this material basis is not the highest value, any more than health is: the highest value is humanity. The best economic basis is of no use if the human foundations collapse.

The subject of abortion is another example of where political decisions are very strongly influenced by religious convictions. And many women perceive that as an unjustified influence on their life situation where they are in a desperate position. We have a clear legal rule for this question, allowing abortion during the first three months of pregnancy, and there was considerable discussion in society before this was formed.

The Church never tires of shaking this political decision and excluding many women in time of need.

Well, of course religious convictions should be able to play a part in this decision. And it is absolutely impossible to see why a law that was decided by a democratic majority, making it legal to carry out abortions in certain circumstances, should not be able to be changed again democratically. Denying that would be in contradiction with democracy.

But that means, then, that there are yet again clear political aims that the Church is pursuing, even though you have just warned against using political influence. In this particular instance, you have a quite concrete political goal: the revocation of the right to early-term abortion?

For many of her goals in social policy, the Church no longer takes the path of one political party, which would be, so to speak, the exclusive representative of the Church's concerns, but, rather, the path of rational argumentation, of political alliances and of political lobbying, which has become perfectly respectable today.

Here is one good example of this. In 1999, Edeltraud Gatterer, a representative of the Austrian parliament, introduced a "report" against euthanasia in the Council of Europe, which was adopted by a large majority. There is a group that since then has been trying to overturn this "Gatterer directive" and to argue for a recommendation of euthanasia that would be valid throughout Europe. It is mainly thanks to the repeated, organized political action by committed Christians that they have so far been unsuccessful and that this directive is still in force. It is quite impossible to see why Christians in a democracy should not, within the normal rules of politics, try to formulate their view, their image of man, and their social choices and also to win majority support for them.

They do that in any case, as voters . . .

Exactly.

. . . and as voters, electing one political party or another, of course they elect and support one political program or another, and thus supposedly its goals—which may or may not be more or less Christian.

That has nothing to do with clericalism or with political Catholicism; it is rather the play of forces in a democracy, through which the points of view of particular social groups are articulated and their influence is brought to bear.

2.2. The Dialogue between Religions

There is a project in Vienna, following the formula of the TV program Tausche Familie *(family swap), that could be called "religion swap". "Religions" are "swapped" on major holidays— that means Christians celebrate Ramadan with Muslims, and, vice versa, Muslims celebrate Christmas with Christians; reactions to this have been divided. Is this the right way toward integration, a project of mutual respect, or disrespect, for the other religion? Can there be religious "try-outs" like that, so as to understand others better?*

I believe that a fundamental presupposition for dialogue between religions is a dialogue between cultures. For there is much in religions that is also culture, tradition. There is never any such thing as "pure religion", but always religion in a certain form. I have heard of this initiative, and I regard it as very positive. There are plans to extend it next year. This time there were twenty-five families, and next year there are to be a hundred. Muslim and Christian families visiting each other. I consider that to be important, because we do have one thing in common—the basis for every dialogue between religions and cultures: the fact that we are all human beings. We have the same basic needs, we have a heart, a brain, eyes and ears, we all need to go to the toilet, and if we are ill, we are all ill the same way. We are men. We live side by side, and hopefully we also live together.

We work together. If I think about the construction site next to us, there are Christians and Muslims there with no distinction between them, working together on the building as a matter of course and . . .

I would guess there are more Muslims there . . .

I would suppose the number of Muslims is not insignificant. In any case, I have never yet asked who belongs to what religion. These are really nice people and good workers. And their basic desires are the same. People want to live in peace, provide food for their families, raise their children, celebrate special occasions. That is a common foundation; in the dialogue between religions, we are talking here about a dialogue of life. Cultivating that is a necessary preliminary, and we should welcome everything that is moving in this direction.

When people talk about integration, the concept of "parallel worlds" comes to mind, a concept that is loaded with fear. They result when people do not want to be integrated at all, do not want to learn the language or get to know the other society. How do you see these "parallel worlds", or could one also say that in any case we all, irrespective of our religion or our beliefs, inhabit parallel worlds?

Upstairs, Downstairs—the play by Johann Nestroy (d. 1862)— shows us that kind of parallel world. A tour of Vienna and its various districts is enough for us to see that we live in parallel worlds. That has always been the case. The question is how strong are the things in common, and how strong the differences? We have had the experience of civil war in our country, a very short one, thank God, yet unfortunately very bloody, with very deep divisions and deep wounds. They were totally parallel worlds. There was the black world, and the red one, and walking the border, crossing the line between the worlds, was often extremely difficult. That has been largely resolved, but of course new parallel worlds are coming into existence. The "brick Bohemians" in Vienna also had their own parallel world; they read their Czech newspapers, met people in Czech associations, and so on. The Turks in Vienna have their Turkish associations. During Advent, I invited all the Turkish associations to an Advent meeting at the archepiscopal palace. That was our first attempt, a very nice meeting. Not everyone came, of course, but many did. It was very interesting for me to note how varied these associations are. We say simply "the Turks". But there are also worlds among the Turks, parallel worlds, different religious orientations, the Alevites, the Muslims, the laity, the secular Turks. There are sports associations, cultural associations, interest groups, and so on. There, too, it turns out, if you look more closely, there are many distinctions. And then we are at the next step: the Islamic world is just as varied, in itself, as the Christian one. The Muslims are inclined to say "the Christians" and to see that globally, so to speak, as the whole of the West.

And vice versa.

And vice versa. It is only when you look more closely that you see that between a Southern Baptist in the U.S. and a Tyrolean Catholic there are profound differences. So we see, with the media also pointing this out to us now, that there are profound differences between Sunni and Shiite Muslims—to the point of having the most bloody conflicts. We should be cautious in our judgments about this.

Let us think how in Europe, a Thirty Years' War set Catholics and Protestants against one another in a terribly bloody conflict. Seeing the differences when you look more closely means also becoming aware that there is not just one Islamic world, but many. Bosnian, Arab and Turkish Muslims have very different cultures. There are the most varied groups within Islam, who in some cases cannot get along with each other any better than is the case in Christian history and within Christianity at present. All that helps us to see that we must not be afraid of these parallel worlds and to approach that reality without fear.

Are most conflicts we have in Europe actually at bottom about entirely other things than religion? When Turkish or Arab youths demonstrate in the suburbs of Paris, then that is after all a social problem in the first instance and not a religious one. Is it not always a matter of power, of economics and underdevelopment, and we translate it into terms of religion, culture, and identity?

It is neither entirely one nor entirely the other. It has been claimed that these conflicts in the suburbs of Paris are not conflicts of religion. The Archbishop of Paris himself said, in a speech in Brussels, that the conflicts in the Paris suburbs involve many Muslims, but that for the Muslim leaders these conflicts are a sign that Muslim spiritual leaders are losing their influence over young people, because they can no longer hold them back, so to speak. The background to this conflict is primarily a social one, the Archbishop said: the hopeless situation of the labor market, in these suburbs, a feeling many of the young people have that they have no future, which drives them to violence. But these conflicts are also not simply social or merely

88

economic ones, rather, they are always a mixture of the most varied elements. Religion can have a calming, integrative effect here, by giving people a sense of belonging, creating communities, and thus working against the mob mentality. Community and a crowd are not the same thing. Religion can, however, have the effect of intensifying a conflict, when it is being misused by people of fundamentalist mentality.

If we look around the world, it is however the case that many Islamic states are the least developed and also the least democratic in the world. Does Islam need an Enlightenment?

Pope Benedict XVI said that very clearly, in his Christmas address to the Curia in 2006: "Islam is confronted by the great challenge that faced Christianity in the Enlightenment." Islam has to deal with this challenge. I believe that one difference for Islam today is that the Enlightenment in Europe in the eighteenth century was a phenomenon of the intellectual elite, and not the great mass of the population. It had an effect on the people beyond the elite only very slowly. The whole nineteenth century was a slow process of secularizing society, until in the twentieth century this really reached the masses, so to speak. Islam today is in a far more dramatic situation, because from a, to some extent, pre-enlightenment era, which for us extended down to the eighteenth century, it is directly faced with a secular world that is not "trickling down" beyond the intellectuals into the broad layer of the population. Through our media culture, secularization comes into every home, everywhere, on everyone's screens, it is omnipresent through Internet and television. That is a far more massive challenge. And I have a great deal of sympathy for the Muslim leaders.

I also tried to have intensive discussions on this subject with the civil and religious leaders in Iran: "How are you dealing with this?" And I certainly had the impression that they are aware of how dramatic the situation is. I shall never forget, in Eşfahan, in the park in front of the famous wooden palace there was a school class—boys and girls were strictly separated, of course—a class of girls who were having drawing lessons there and were supposed to be drawing this palace. I took the liberty of talking to these girls, and that worked quite well in English. We then tried, with an interpreter, to have a discussion; they were all dressed completely in black, with the chador and full-length long black robes, but in practically every case you could see blue jeans underneath. That, for me, was a symbol of how much tension there is in the situation in Islam. Surviving and overcoming this conflict between the modern world and tradition is a tremendous challenge. And besides that, there is a dramatic tension that I very clearly sensed in Iran, in that they do not envisage a separation of church and state, of religion and politics, in Islam. In modern society, however, this is indispensable.

And will Islam be able to cope with the economic challenge of our era? When you see now how China and India are rising to be the dominant powers, economic powers, in Asia—will the countries where Islam is dominant not end up falling behind yet again, precisely because religion is an obstacle here? That seems to me to be the great challenge for Islam, and the Pope addressed this point in a few clear words—not at all in the sense of malicious criticism, but, rather, in a shared concern for the future of those countries. We are of course convinced that religion is good for people and is important for them, but religion can also be an obstacle and can harm them, as we know from our own history.

One of the subjects of the Pope's speech at Regensburg that caused such a stir was the subject of faith and reason. Is the relation between them different in Islam from what it is in Christianity?

I can only give a partial answer to that question. The Pope said quite clearly in his Regensburg speech that that is the great challenge for religion generally. He said quite clearly, and he is convinced of this, that Christianity, which sets the Logos at the center of things—"In the beginning was the Word", in the beginning was reason—is better adapted to this relationship between religion and reason than other religions are. This evaluation needs to be discussed, of course, and that discussion is age-old.

The Pope's Regensburg speech reminded me of Nicholas of Cusa, the great German scholar, a fifteenth-century cardinal, who was for a while Bishop of Brixen and then occupied an important position in the Curia in Rome, perhaps the greatest philosopher and thinker of the fifteenth century. He wrote a book called *De pace fidei*, "On the Peace of Faith" or "On Peace in Religion". He has a council of religions taking place in heaven—most interesting—and the religions then known to him come forward and discuss reason and religion with Christ. It is not surprising that in this heavenly council Christianity then proves to be the most rational religion; but the most remarkable thing is that Nicholas of Cusa knew the Qur'an quite well, actually very well for his time. He used a Latin translation of the Qur'an and wrote a great thick tome on the Qur'an, the *Cribratio Alkorani*, that is to say the "Scrutiny of the Qur'an", or "The Qur'an Sifted". He made an intensive study of Islam. He was not familiar with the East Asian religions.

The question of the rationality of religion is a fundamental subject, which even classical philosophy—Plato,

Aristotle, and the Romans—discussed. The Christian tradition took it up right from the beginning; Augustine (d. 430) did so in his great work *The City of God*. But Islam, too, in its great springtime in the Middle Ages, attempted philosophically to present Islam as the rational religion. Up to the present day, there are Muslim scholars who emphasize that. If, for instance, you read the letter of the thirty-eight Muslim scholars who replied to the Pope's Regensburg speech, they emphasize that there is no contradiction between the Qur'an and reason.

It is not, of course, so completely simple as that. Martin Luther (d. 1546) called reason a whore and set it in opposition to faith. Reason can be seduced and seduces man. Luther was therefore quite right to point out: "Take care, much that is irrational can be perpetrated with the reason." Paul himself talks about the foolishness of God, which is wiser than all the reason of men. Religion is always concerned likewise with the irrational, with the ecstatic, with enthusiasm, which goes beyond the bounds of reason.

Immanuel Kant, in his late work *Religion within the Boundaries of Mere Reason*, tried to reduce religion to reason entirely. He pruned away everything that stood beyond the border of reason, so to speak. He had to cut away a great deal—the doctrine of the Trinity, for example, is unreasonable. Even the Incarnation of God will not really hold its own in the face of reason. Hence, the relation between reason and religion is a little bit more complicated than the way it is presented in the Regensburg speech, and the Pope, of course, knows that, too. We also need the element that goes beyond reason. Ultimately, we are most clearly confronted by this question: What is the relationship between reason and love? Love has its reason, as Pascal says, "Le coeur a ses raisons." The heart has a reason of its own. And the exciting thing is, in all probability, that the proper balance between reason and the heart, between reason and love, is the primary thing that allows man to be complete. If he is only rational, then ultimately he is being irrational; and if he responds only to the weight of love, the "pondus amoris", as Augustine says, he is in danger once again of being irrational.

Let us stay with Islam and the arguments associated with it. These questions are going to be among the most urgent for us in the coming years. And many of these questions are in fact not of an intellectual nature, but are everyday questions—and then again, questions about symbols. One of these "symbols" made for some headlines last Christmas: no Christmas cribs were set up in Italian kindergartens, and no Christmas carols were sung, because there are also many Muslim children there. What do you say about that kind of development?

I regard it as sheer nonsense. There is no "religion-free" culture. Wherever we go in the world, our cultures are impregnated with religion. If I go to Indonesia—I was in Indonesia, that time, after the tsunami—I encounter the Islamic culture of that country everywhere. If I travel to Sri Lanka, then everywhere I encounter the fact that the majority of that country is Buddhist. And in Candy, the principal shrine of Sri Lanka, a precious relic—one of the Buddha's teeth—is revered. The pilgrims come to that temple in thousands to pray there, to bring sacrifice, and to seek help from above. You cannot remove Buddhism from Sri Lankan culture or from the country's folklore, and you cannot remove the Christian heritage from European culture. You would then be destroying that culture, and our museums would also have to be cleared out, since it could also be uncomfortable for a Muslim, if he went into the Prado or the

Museum of Fine Arts in Vienna and found nothing but Christian scenes. Then we would also have to get rid of Raphael, Michelangelo, and Velázquez.

So is this a kind of misunderstanding of integration?

It is a complete misunderstanding of what integration means. Integration cannot be opposed to identity! Identity means belonging, and one of the most profound sources of a sense of belonging, besides the family, is religion. The hymns I sang in church as a boy I will remember all my life. They are a part of my identity. Why should I renounce that in order to be open to other people?

When we invited the Turkish associations to join us in Advent, we quite deliberately sang some Advent hymns. We said to the Turks, a great number of whom have meanwhile become Austrian citizens and are our fellow countrymen, our neighbors: "We simply want to show you how we celebrate Advent." There was an Advent wreath, and we sang Advent hymns, with content that is unacceptable for Islam—that is, about the divine child in the crib and God becoming man. The Cross was hanging there, which is a matter of course with us. I am not going to cover it over or take it down because I have Muslim guests in the house. For they are coming to me as guests. But I will not demand that they remove the symbols of their religion if I go to their house as a guest. A good part of identity consists in religious identity. It is therefore completely mistaken to say that the crosses must be taken away so that the Muslims should not be bothered by them. Then we would have to be constantly switching, so to speak—whenever a Muslim comes, we hang up a crescent moon; when Christians are there, a cross. Culture does not work that way.

There are people who think the simple alternative is not to hang anything up at all.

Yes, and make life colorless. "Zero reports" all around. That cannot be. I cannot remove church spires from Austrian life. I have nothing at all against there being a mosque in Vienna, with a minaret. I would of course be very happy if church spires were also allowed in Muslim countries. I have experienced that in Indonesia. In Jakarta there is a large, magnificent mosque, to which I paid an official visit, and opposite, on the other side of the street, is the Catholic cathedral. At Christmas, the Muslim parking-lot attendants keep places free so that the Catholics can go to midnight Mass; and on the other hand, on the Islamic festivals the cardinal crosses the street to the mosque and visits the Muslims. That is what I call mutual acceptance of identity.

Is it really as simple, then, as merely having to keep parking places free for one another? Look at the other side, at the way religious wars develop out of distant territorial conflicts. People then talk about fighting and killing in the name of God. What is it about the great religions that allows them to be so incredibly misused?

We have enough examples of living together successfully. For a long time, Lebanon was an example of this, though of course there have been explosions of violence in its history, time and again—even violence between the religions. The old Austria, the monarchy, was an exemplary instance of religious coexistence. It worked. In Bosnia, up until the war, people lived next door to one another in peace, Muslims, Orthodox, and Catholics, as good neighbors. What happened there?

I believe it is almost always ideological propaganda, the "divide et impera" of the ancient Romans, "Divide and rule!", inciting groups of people against one another so as to be able to rule them better. Fanning the flames of conflict so as to get one's hands on power is an old and dreadful method in politics, an abuse. I am convinced that most cases of religious conflict are of that kind. Very often they are also brought about socially—Northern Ireland is a typical example, where the English rulers, Protestants or Anglicans, oppressed the Catholics for centuries. This social, societal injustice, the inequality in dealing with one religion in comparison with the other, one social class in comparison with another, very often sooner or later leads to conflict, such as we are familiar with from Northern Ireland, for instance. If it once becomes as firmly entrenched as is the case there, then it can take decades for such a conflict to be overcome.

If we look at the Near East, however, we have the sense that it is not possible, even after many generations?

France and Germany, "hereditary enemies". I shall never forget when I came to France in 1968 as a student in our Dominican house of studies. On one of my first days there, I was walking in the garden with an old French father, and he suddenly started to cry and said to me, "Can you imagine this? My grandfather fought in the war of 1870, when Germany captured Paris, and the German Empire was proclaimed at Versailles. My father took part in the First World War, Germany against France. I was a prisoner of war in Germany for five years during the Second World War. And now you stroll with me, quite peacefully. Can you understand that I am overcome by that?" I shall never forget that moment.

Can one imagine, today, a war breaking out again between France and Germany? We never know, the old demons are never really asleep. For now, they are buried under a thick layer of mutual interests, and may they stay buried. Conflicts can be resolved. An old Jewish friend, Rabbi Schneier from New York with roots in Vienna, was present at the unforgettable Kosovo Conference, when shortly before the beginning of the war all the religions of Kosovo met in Vienna—unfortunately, this peace conference was unsuccessful. Rabbi Schneier said something I shall never forget: "All wars end sometime. No war has ever lasted forever." Even the conflict between Israel and Palestine will end sometime. How will it end, when will it end? We do not know. We only know that it will end sometime. The Thirty Years' War ended, after thirty years.

Is the radicalization of religion likewise a result of globalization?

Globalization is certainly a most significant occurrence, because through modern technology, the current economy, and the shrinking of distances, we are experiencing everything as much closer. In the Middle Ages we did not notice a conflict in Samarkand. Today, we notice a conflict in Afghanistan, which is, so to speak, quite close to us; the refugees from Afghanistan are here with us, and there are European soldiers in Afghanistan. What happens there affects our domestic policy. The economic development of China directly affects us, and not merely through the shipments of porcelain, as in the baroque era. This globalization is making even religious conflicts omnipresent. But I am convinced that even religious conflicts have an expiration date. There will always be conflicts, but they will not always be the same ones. The wars of religion in Europe, which after all shaped European history from the sixteenth century until practically into the nineteenth century, are a thing of the past as a phenomenon within Christianity today.

Does that mean that we need not be afraid of Islam?

How does the saying go, "Dying of fear is still dying", is it? I believe we ought not to be afraid of Islam; we should see the Muslims as our neighbors, as people, first and foremost, and meet them as brothers and sisters in the family of man. They have a religion that is different from our religion. Perhaps they remind us that we have somewhat thoughtlessly discarded our religion. Perhaps they remind us, too, that religion should be taken a little bit more seriously than secularized Europe is doing at the moment. They present us with difficulties, because they are often more inflexible in their religiousness, in their convictions, and perhaps also less tolerant than we are. But having said this, we have no need to be afraid of Islam.

We must see, unemotionally, that coexistence with Islam is not easy, is a great challenge, but it is possible. And we must show more solidarity with Christians in Muslim countries. It is quite painful to see that so-called Christian Europe cares very little at all about the Christians in the Near East and Middle East. For centuries, the European states were the powers protecting the Christians in the Near East. The Habsburg monarchy was the power protecting the Melkites in Lebanon and Syria. The French were the power protecting the Maronites. Today, the Christians in the Near East feel abandoned by us. Where is Christian solidarity? If the Muslims sensed more clearly that we were watching out for our brothers and sisters in the faith, they would probably also have more respect for us.

Would that not also constitute a source of further conflicts?

No, if anything, it would probably tend to strengthen cooperation. The point is not that we intervene with armed force, but that we send clear signals of solidarity. Think about the fact that there are a million Christians in Saudi Arabia who are not allowed to practice their religion in any way. America and Europe are merely looking on, simply on account of the petrodollar: that is scandalous!

What might that kind of peaceful indication look like?

There should be no European or American politician who enters into talks with Saudi Arabia without this being one of the subjects. It is simply unacceptable that a million people, who are there to some extent for slave labor or to perform the most menial kind of work, are simply prevented from practicing their religion. That has to be addressed! And what are Muslims to think of Christian politicians if they never raise the issue?

That will not be raised until there is no more oil there . . . ?

Exactly!

Soon, then.

Yes, that will be quite soon.

Chapter 3

The Cross along with the Church

3.1. Would Jesus Be in the Church Today?

Can someone be a Christian without a church? There are so many people who work with the sick, the elderly, with homeless people and the marginalized in our society, who are there for these people and, thus, living Christian ideas in their most unadulterated form. Many of them, however, are not Catholic, nor do they have any use for the Church's rules and regulations. Nonetheless, I ask myself: Are they not the better Christians, at any rate, better than very many who go to church on Sundays?

Yes, and no. I often hear that: "I'm not a bigot, I don't go to church, but I am a good Christian." And then I say again, "Which of us is a good Christians is something Christ will ultimately decide; we all have to appear before his throne of judgment." He will judge whether, in his eyes, I have been a good Christian. Part of being a good Christian, in the human, earthly order of things, is going to church to worship. For that is actually, as they used to say, our Christian duty. And part of it, of course, is also keeping the commandments of loving God and one's neighbor and not behaving like a scoundrel or a slave-driver. That is the human order of things. According to the human, earthly order of things, of which the Church order is also a part, I would have to answer someone who says, "I don't need any church in order to be a good Christian": That is not right. In order to be a Christian in the sense of our earthly pilgrimage, you need a church, and you need a community. "A single Christian is not a Christian", wrote Tertullian (d. 220), an early Christian writer. That is to say, you cannot be a Christian on your own.

Another question is, "How do I stand before God?" In the Gospel of Matthew, chapter 25, Jesus is talking about the final judgment. There, he does not ask, "Have you gone to church on Sundays? Have you paid your parish contributions? Have you obeyed your bishop?" There, the judge says only, "I was sick, and you visited me. I was naked, and you clothed me. I was in prison, and you visited me. I was hungry, and you gave me food. I was thirsty, and you gave me drink." Then those concerned will ask, "When did we see you naked and clothe you?" and so on. And then Jesus replies, "Whatever you did for the least of my brothers, you did for me." They had not perceived that at all. They simply did it. In the judgment of God, no doubt, the critical point will not be whether I have fulfilled all the Church's commandments, but whether I have lived love. There are, no doubt, many people who are not part of the visible community of the Church, and in that sense are not Christians, but to whom Christ will say, "Come, O blessed of my Father, for the kingdom of heaven is prepared for you."

Yet since we are pilgrims on earth, I still have to say to our dear former Christians: You cannot make things quite so easy for yourselves by saying, "I don't need the Church", since the passage is not so simple. Renouncing all the help and support, all safe-conduct on the path, that I find in the community of faith is somewhat irresponsible. I think many people in our society are dealing irresponsibly with the capital of their lives, with what we need by way of spirituality in order to pass along the path of life, when they say, "I don't need the Church."

In fact, many people—I will call them the "seeking generation" for now—want this search and the fascination of a higher power, which they associate with positive values like love, peace, and humanity. Different, negative things are associated with the Church: inflexible rules and dogmas, restrictions, obligations, and even anxiety and fear. What is going wrong with communication here? What is going wrong with the public relations, so that God is in fact love, but the Church is the problem?

I would like to compare that to some extent with a situation we come across quite frequently these days, one that is often very painful—that of children of divorced parents. The mother has the task of bringing them up, and the father sees the children once every two weeks. The father spoils the children, when they come to him every two weeks; he is the generous one and does not have to take on all the trouble of everyday life with the children. The mother, in addition to her role as mother, has to take on the father's role in daily life. That means she has to be twice as strict, has to carry out a double share of their upbringing. And of course, mother is the bad one and father the good one.

That comparison does not add up . . .

Mother Church . . .

. . . because that would mean that God is off the hook, because he is not there in everyday life.

That is actually a very good objection—as with every comparison, my comparison obviously has its weak points. I do not think it is entirely wrong, since any comparison has just one point in which it holds, and the point here is that the Church, in this society, is something like a single mother. The "fathers", who have far less concrete responsibility, are what is offered by our society. Mother Church has the unpleasant task of constantly saying to us, in our everyday affairs, "But you ought to do that this way, and you are not allowed that, and you must do this ..." Exactly as a single mother has to do in the daily task of bringing up her children. The competition facing the Church is enormous. The offers that say, "Take it easy", "Have a good time", "Don't worry about it", are multitudinous and far more tempting than the sober, strict choice offered by the Church, which challenges you, "You have to get up on Sunday and go to church, and you have to go to confession and take a look at what is not in order in your life." These are all things people do not like to hear, and the alternatives offer something far more enjoyable. The Church is not the only one in the marketplace.

Prebendary Koch (Cologne) says this on the subject: "Most people regard the Church as a supermarket. People pick up the interesting offers—kindergarten, school, special worship services—and leave the Commandments and the pope; they pay their church tax at the cashier and expect prompt service. Then they go into the next shop and see what astrology, Buddhism, and psychotherapy have to offer today. And the following week, they make these decisions all over again." Does this image fit the current situation?

Perfectly. I think one could not put it better. As a psychotherapist or psychologist, however—I have also studied that a little—one would have to say that this is a dangerous approach to life, because ultimately it gives no structure. It leaves you with a rather ambivalent attitude that cannot make you happy, either. Why is it we know from our own experience or from observation, that a good upbringing, a loving upbringing, is also a strict upbringing? Because it gives structure, because it strengthens your backbone, because it prepares you for a life that does not shift like a jellyfish, but where you can walk upright. And in what it offers you, the Church is of course in the same position as parents who are not willing to let their children get into every "Playmobil" or video game and who set limits.

But how can the Church raise her profile now in the market for life coaching and the search for meaning? How can I reach the believer who also goes to the astrologer, to the life coach, the health guru, and the psychotherapist? How can I say, "Have a look at what I can offer"? The German "Lufthansa" airline, for example, had the slogan, "We keep the skies open". Is not that really the slogan of the Church?

That is a nice slogan, but the slogan should not be too much at the service of vague, general emotions.

What is the Church's slogan today?

I am convinced that it can only be the offer of Jesus himself. At times of crisis like this, you always have to ask: What is the core? What is the essence? In the course of her history, the Church has made the strongest gains in times of crisis when she has recalled the essence. Take Benedict of Nursia (d. 547) and the monastic movement in a period of chaos, when people recalled what "following Jesus" really meant. The most memorable instance, for us, is perhaps the thirteenth century with Francis (d. 1226) and Dominic (d. 1221): the rise of towns, the emergence of the marketplace, in fact, the first steps toward our modern economy—and into this came a way of life with a clear and definite shape, the movement for evangelical poverty, the mendicant friars, the Franciscan movement. The gospel as alternative. In the twentieth century, perhaps the most obvious example is that of Mother Teresa (d. 1997).

The most interesting thing is that as soon as the gospel can be seen in a clearly defined, concrete manner, it speaks to people right across religious divisions and challenges them, because—and this is the most profound conviction of the Christian faith—the gospel of Jesus has truly revealed God's innermost heart. This is what our God is like, and this is how he wants us to live. Wherever people encounter the gospel, there God is, in our so vague and often banal, trivial, and uncommitted times. Suddenly we feel, "That's exactly it, that is exactly what is necessary." That is why I do not see the Church's path in successful slogans like, "keep the skies open", but in forms in which the gospel can be read. These are always concrete people, groups, communities.

The very first people who followed Jesus were John and Andrew, when he was down by the Jordan with John the Baptist. They were walking behind him, and Jesus turned around and asked them, "What do you seek?"—and they wanted to know from him, "Teacher, where are you staying?" At that, he said to them, "Come and see." And they went with him, and saw where he was staying, and remained with him for the day. "Come and see!" There is nothing more urgently needed in Christianity than a place, and especially people, in which and in whom it can be seen. So I do not concern myself about the Church's PR. Jesus did not give us the mission of making as much and as good PR as we can; rather, he said, "Preach the gospel, the good news." That must become visible and audible.

3.2. Guilt and Sin

Another difficulty that many people have with the Church is the fundamental importance of guilt in the Catholic Church, the significance of sin: "The Church invented sin in order to wield power over us", many say. What would you reply to that?

I believe there is some truth in that, but that is a one-sided way of putting it. I would say this: "The Church discovered sin, or—in the literal sense—uncovered it, exposed it." In a certain sense, one could say that the pagan world is not yet aware of sin. In a certain sense, it relates directly to nature, to its environment, and even to the divinity, and not until the law given on Sinai did the Jewish law and the Ten Commandments expose evil. The Apostle Paul expressed that very pointedly. Sin did not come into the world through the law, but people were thereby made aware of it. And that also holds good for our experience in life. It was only the encounter with grace and with God's law that I first became aware of evil as a reality in my life. To that extent, we could truly say that the Church discovered sin, that she revealed it—not the Church as an institution, but the God of the Old Testament, the God of Christ, Jesus Christ himself.

To make this clear, I will take an example from the Gospels, the parable of the Good Samaritan—we all know that. A man on his way from Jericho to Jerusalem is attacked by robbers. It is the usual road frequently traveled by pilgrims through the desert to Jerusalem. The robbers attack him. He is left lying there, gravely wounded. Two clerics from the temple, a Levite and a priest, come past, but they are in a hurry and go on. A foreigner comes along, sees him, and turns aside to him. Through this parable, Jesus was actually exposing something that perhaps was not so noticeable before: the bypassing of a neighbor in distress, who needs me. And since Jesus first told this story, it has been like a thorn. We cannot get rid of this thorn. Jesus revealed the love of one's neighbor and the failures to love one's neighbor. In a certain sense, he has planted a thorn in our flesh and has thereby brought something into the world that had not yet been given it so clearly. And this has naturally produced a "bad conscience" as well, because it has revealed that we prefer to bypass our neighbor.

But what is the Church doing about it now? The Church, or Jesus, discovered sin, exposed it. In the realm of interpersonal relations, people would say that a bad conscience is a poor basis for a partnership. A good many people have the feeling that it is precisely this bad conscience which is the basis of their relationship with the Church. Who wishes to enter into such a relationship of his own free will?

Again, that is not true. I believe that a bad conscience is a conscience that is working properly. Let us for the moment take an extreme instance. If we say a person is without any conscience, then we are really saying he is inhuman. He lacks something essential to being human. If we say a person has a sensitive conscience, then we feel that is something very positive. Someone comes to me and says, "I beg your pardon, I slammed the door too hard just now." We feel that is something very good. Someone is being so sensitive that he reacts even to little things and notices that there was something not quite right there, something that should have been done differently.

A sensitive conscience is something very fine, from the human point of view. A person with no conscience is inhuman. Well, as with all positive things, there is of course a distorted form of this. That is a false sense of guilt. Distinguishing false feelings of guilt from proper feelings of guilt is an important matter in spirituality. I think we often make the mistake of identifying guilt feelings as a whole with false feelings of guilt. Woe to the person who no longer has any genuine feelings of guilt! It is bad for the person who has false feelings of guilt. False feelings of guilt do not arise naturally; rather, they are imposed, instilled, inculcated in a person and are also dangerous. They are also something to be overcome. One of the greatest tasks of lived spirituality is the distinction between genuine and false feelings of guilt.

Many people who have enjoyed a Catholic upbringing or attended a Catholic boarding school give a quite different account of this time and of the way guilt feelings were treated: guilt feelings as a means of exercising control. Either you believe, or you will have to pay the price.

I think we are taking too easy a way out if we describe that as a phenomenon of the Church. It is, unfortunately, a very widespread human phenomenon to work on false guilt feelings. The withdrawal of love as a threat. How many parents make that threat to their children; in how many relationships does that happen! Being valued only on the basis of achievement: "If you work hard, I like you; if you do not live up to my expectations, I do not like you." Those are the elements that can build up false guilt feelings, from which people suffer dreadfully. I see the task of the gospel, which is indeed the basis of the Church, as being to bring us to genuine feelings of guilt and set us free from false guilt feelings.

Genuine feelings of guilt are enormously beneficial, if—and this is the decisive point—they develop concurrently with an awareness of grace. On this point the gospel is unrivaled in transmitting a sensitivity to and knowledge about genuine feelings of guilt. The classic example is found in the Gospel of John, chapter 8. A woman who has been caught in the act of adultery is brought to Jesus. The older men all stand around this woman, who is lying on the ground in front of Jesus, and accuse her and say to Jesus, "What do you say? The law demands that this woman be stoned." We all know his answer. Jesus remains silent. He writes in the sand with his finger. They insist, and he straightens up and looks at them and says, "Let him who is without sin among you be the first to throw a stone at her." That has almost become proverbial. Jesus does not say, "The law is wrong", but he confronts each person with his own history.

Another example, December 2006. A seriously ill Italian man, who had required intensive nursing for decades, who for decades had advocated euthanasia and had wanted to have his respirator switched off. And after long discussions, protests, and public commotion, that is what actually happened. As a result, he was not allowed a Church burial. Many thought the Church was lacking in mercy. Where was that mercy?

I have to admit—and this may be interpreted as an excuse—that I know too little about the circumstances. All I know is the brief item in our newspapers, about the burial being denied. In cases like this, I always say that I would like to know exactly what the situation was: What really happened? Was it a case of genuine euthanasia? Was it actively or passively assisted suicide? Those two have to be quite clearly distinguished. And then, what was really the position of the Church? I am quite willing to talk about the problem as such. On this particular case, I would not venture to say anything without specific knowledge.

I will clarify this with the question of guilt feelings in a quite simple example. A dear school friend of mine is head of a urology department, so he also has a lot to do with patients suffering from cancer, and he tells me it sometimes happens that the family of a cancer patient say, "Doctor, look, Grandma is suffering so dreadfully. Couldn't she be given a bit of help, so that this suffering will be shorter?" And he says, "Well, kill your Grandma off yourself!" And suddenly the question is quite clear. Is it a matter of actively killing someone or of allowing him to die? Actively helping to die means taking the initiative to kill someone, with an injection for instance, which will inevitably bring death. Passive help means forgoing further application of medical technology so as to make it possible for things to run their natural course, so as to allow someone to die who is in the last stage of his illness. Passively helping someone to die is to be judged quite differently, from a moral point of view, from actively helping him to die. In the case of the Italian man, it would need to be clarified exactly what it was ...

I did not want to go into the question of euthanasia now, but the question of mercy. Even if one were to conclude that it is a grave sin, where is the mercy, the grace of the Church?

The grace of the Church? Grace does not belong to the Church; rather, it is in God's hand. The Church has never made a judgment as to whether someone stands before God in a state of grace or not. It is even the explicit teaching of the Church that not even the pope can determine that. The pope cannot solemnly declare that this or that person has certainly gone to hell—that is, has not found grace before

God, has squandered his last share of grace. That is God's affair alone. The Church is part of the next to the last order of things. And in the next to the last order, in which we all are in this world, we know that there is no final certainty.

When someone is denied a Church burial, that does not mean that grace is being denied that person. God gives grace. As long as he is on earth—and the trip to the cemetery is the last journey on earth—a man is still in the earthly order of things. Whether someone is thrown into a mass grave as a murderer, as is the case in a good many countries where the death penalty is in force, or whether he is given an honorable burial says nothing at all about God's judgment concerning that person. That is the world's judgment. The Church's judgment is still part of the earthly pilgrimage. No priest and no bishop, in denying someone a sacrament or a burial, can thereby say, "I am denying you grace"! He can only say, "According to the Church's order on this earth, this is not allowed or not possible." We have no authority— thank God—over how God judges it. God is not bound by us. We are tied to an ecclesiastical order that we interpret more strictly or more broadly, but we cannot skip it completely.

With many of the positions the Church takes on socio-political questions, that is, the attitude of the Church to questions and difficulties in our lives, that is of course also the point that many people criticize, and consequently their faith and the Church part company. Many people say, "God—yes; faith—yes; but Church— no. Because her teachings are naive, because they do not give me answers to my questions. And she does not necessarily have anything to do with my communications with God or with my idea of God, my conversation with God." Is that okay? Can you understand that people have such difficulties with the Church's views on various socio-political subjects that they say, "My faith they cannot take away from me, but I cannot go along the Church's path"?

Here I would again make a distinction or ask in turn, "What do I understand by 'Church'?" What we understand by "Church" is more often than not the so-called official church, and by this we mean concretely the episcopal Church, that is, the bishops, or Rome, and their declarations. I cannot blame anybody for seeing the Church like that, since that is how she does in fact appear. But like everything else in the world, the Church is in fact a complex reality, consisting not merely of the institutional aspect but also the spiritual aspect. The Church is a community of faith, a spiritual reality and at the same time an institutional reality. Time and again, we tend to want to make a strict division between these things. People say, "Yes, I am in agreement with the spiritual dimension of the Church and, in any event, with the gospel. I find that quite lovely. Believing and praying—that's all fine with me, but I do not want anything institutional." And yet even man's soul is not to be found without a body. The gospel is not to be found without the institution. The spiritual dimension of the Church is not to be separated from the human, institutional side. I think that is what gives offense.

But why does the Church make it so difficult for people in this respect?

Because reality makes it so difficult for people. Just imagine: a young left-wing intellectual experiences a conversion. Perhaps he has read the biography of a saint or has met some awe-inspiring Christian figure, has had a strong inner experience, and suddenly sees the Church in quite a new light. Filled with joy, he discovers: "It is tremendous what is there, the treasures of the saints, the liturgy: that is something tremendous." He has a strong personal experience of grace. Then on Sunday he goes to Mass and sees Mrs. X and Mr. Y, he hears the gossip afterward in the parish coffee room, the parish priest lisps, the sermon is poor, and suddenly he says to himself, "For God's sake, what have I come to?" That is not a fabrication; there are stories like that.

That is the moment when the devil intervenes. I recommend people read something that describes this exquisitely: C. S. Lewis' famous *Screwtape Letters*. An incident like that happens there. The Church—this miserable community with all its failings. Suddenly you see Mrs. X, "Who is in no way better than my neighbor, who never goes to church. On the contrary, perhaps even. . . . The Vicar has strange ideas, and actually no sense of the mystical, which I have experienced." And, and, and. Then suddenly this challenge comes into one's mind. This Church is something so glorious, and so dreadfully human. How do you resolve that? You can try to resolve it by separating the visible Church from the invisible. Then the visible Church becomes even more pitiful, and the invisible one evaporates, vaporizes. It only works—as the Second Vatican Council said—if you see the Church as that "one complex reality that comes together from divine and human elements" (*Lumen Gentium*, no. 8). Divinity is in this Church in human clothing. And that is, and will always remain, the scandal in this Church. Even the best pope, the most sympathetic bishop, and the most fantastic parish priest cannot do away with that.

That means that God is not the problem, but people. Or, as many people like to put it, "It's the ground crew who cause the problem"?

We have to combine that with Jesus' words in the first saying in the Gospel, "Repent, and believe in the gospel" (Mk 1:15). *Metanoia*, the revision of one's thinking, in mind and heart, is the decisive thing. Our view of Mrs. X and Mr. Y, alongside whom our newly converted left-wing intellectual suddenly finds himself at Sunday Mass, is changed. He discovers, "This God, who is here in the bread, whom I receive here in this humble form of the Eucharist, loves me and accepts me, with all my cleverness. But before him, I too am pitiful, and perhaps I have not yet discovered what treasures there are within Mrs. X and Mr. Y and have not yet overcome my prejudices that 'Catholics' are just that way."

It is always good to remove prejudices. But are they really merely prejudices? Are Catholics not really like that? Are there not such an infinite number of chances there that the Church has missed?

There are an infinity of those, and that is a great sorrow. Sometimes one bears this sorrow oneself, because one has failed to grasp the opportunity, find the words or take the right approach. Why do we not talk about the mystery of all mysteries on Sunday? Why do a good many parish priests not venture to tell children that Jesus is really coming to them? If that is not so, then we would do better to go to some civil religion, where people hold civic ceremonies. But the mystery is gone then. Karl Rahner (d. 1984) was quite right in saying, "Only the mystery consoles." Even if one does not think about it every Sunday or go to church every Sunday. It is from this mystery of faith that the Church lives in her inmost heart; it is why she is renewed in spite of all the humanness, why she has not been destroyed by parish priests and bishops in two thousand years but is renewed from generation to generation, and, in truth, profoundly.

I may show that with another example. I went with our seminarians from Vienna on our annual summer holiday pilgrimage to Italy. We traveled from Aquileia by way of Padua and Loreto to San Giovanni Rotondo. At the start, I said to them, "We are now going to sample a kind of cross-section through the centuries." Loreto was one of our stops: there the house from Nazareth is revered, where it all started when a virgin, a young woman from Nazareth, said Yes to an incredible message. That was the midpoint of our pilgrimage. And then we glanced through the centuries: the Patriarchate of Aquileia, from which Christianity was brought to the whole of southern Austria, the early phase of evangelization. Then Padua, the Middle Ages: Anthony, that incredible, charismatic saint, who in the few years of his life turned the whole of Europe upside down, almost more than Saint Francis, or at least as much. And then, finally, San Giovanni Rotondo in the twentieth century, Padre Pio, who died in 1968, whom I personally experienced. Today, seven million people a year go on pilgrimage to his grave in that isolated village. And obviously, again and again, new in every century, there is the same vitality. The Church is simply not to be snuffed out. Not even by us clergy.

3.3. Divorce—and Then?

Let us stay with the pertinent questions concerning the Church with which many believers have difficulties. The subject of weddings, for example. There is an enormous reduction in the number of Church weddings, a dramatic decline. It is certainly a matter of coming to a binding decision that will last a whole life long. But is this question not also a point where the Church must take a completely unequivocal stand about how to proceed? What you said yourself at Thomas Klestil's funeral has resolved a great deal and made a big difference—your speech was understood as a cautious opening. Why not say it again clearly and distinctly? Why no remarriage for divorced people?

Things are more complicated, and in our present age it is hard to make people aware of complex matters. But I think we are succeeding. Let us stay with marriage, because it is the basic form of human cohabitation, and we all have fathers and mothers, or we would not be here. If this family unit was good, things went well for us; many are not so lucky, and they have to cope with it. I really cannot imagine it is right, as we read recently, that 60 percent of marriages in Vienna end in divorce.

The most recent figures were indeed that high: in large cities like Vienna, a more than 60 percent divorce rate, in rural areas somewhat less.

That means the question of how do we deal with broken and new relationships concerns practically everyone. For those people whose marriage does not fail at least know someone around them, among their relations or their children or friends, whose marriage has broken up. It is thus valid to say that the Church must be more aware of this problem. That is why, for the past several years, together with the priests of our diocese, I have developed a five-point method, a kind of questionnaire, to see what the situation really is.

For one thing cannot happen, even though it is often demanded: that the Church should simply recognize the collapse of one relationship and the existence of another. There are two reasons why that is impossible. First, Jesus said, "Whoever leaves his wife and takes another commits adultery. And if a wife leaves her husband and takes another, she commits adultery." These are not comfortable words, but Jesus said them clearly and unequivocally. The second thing, however, is that in a divorce and remarriage there are always several people involved. And a liberal attitude on the part of the Church on one side may lead to people who find the separation painful feeling they have been betrayed by the Church. That is why I have said: Let us look at it first of all from the point of view of the gospel, to see what the Church has to consider. She must consider the weakest. Jesus always looked to the little ones, the weak ones, and fought against their being oppressed, despised, or forgotten. Who are the weakest, when a marriage collapses?

In most cases it is the children, if there are any in a marriage.

I have repeatedly said that the first point is the question: How are the children? Whenever someone's marriage has collapsed, and there is a new relationship, and they want to have the Church's blessing at all costs, the first question for me is: How about the children from the first marriage? Have you unloaded your conflicts onto the shoulders of the children? Or have you taken care that the children suffer as little harm as possible? Are the children being torn apart by mind-games? Are you making hostages of the children in this conflict? As long as that is the case, a Church blessing for the new marriage is a mockery in the eyes of the children. And the children must say to themselves, So that is how the Church treats our suffering!

The second point: I hear many complaints about the Church's severity toward divorced people who have remarried. I hear very few voices raised on behalf of the spouse who has been left. And in our society they are legion: women who are no longer young enough to find another spouse, men who cannot come to terms with the divorce and let themselves go downhill. What happens to the spouse who remains? Those are the ones the Church ought to be looking at first.

Third point: How does the story of blame and responsibility look? Has the history of responsibility been worked out? Are there at least some beginnings of reconciliation with the first spouse? Or are they stumbling into a new partnership and carrying along the baggage of unresolved guilt from the preceding one? It is vitally necessary to deal with this, simply from the point of view of the human success of a relationship. How can any blessing be given before all that has been cleared up?

But that means we might as well forget it, there can never be a Church blessing for the remarried, since these questions can never be entirely cleared up. As is well known, there are always several truths, in any case three: mine, yours, and the right one. Answering the questions you have just posed could take a lifetime.

Yes and no.

Whether a child has been hurt by the parents' divorce, and how that will be expressed, we get to know that perhaps over decades. These questions may have far-reaching and dramatic consequences— but can they in fact be the basis for the Church's attitude to new partnerships? That will not help a single child!

I have two more points, and then we will come back to that. The fourth point is, there are married couples who quite deliberately stay together, making great sacrifices, because they have promised that to each other and to God. How does the Church deal with them? If she is always saying only, "Oh, those poor divorced people who have remarried!" Where is the word of consolation and encouragement for those people, who have perhaps gone through many deep valleys and have remained faithful?

And finally, fifth and last, what is decisive is: How do we stand before God in our new relationship? Even if we can deceive ourselves and fool each other, we cannot lie to God. In plain language, that means that an "in-and-out" blessing is not really helpful. If the Church simply rubber-stamps divorces and remarriages as the civil law does, she is not doing any good to people. She is then betraying her ministry to men, not being a mother and spiritual adviser. In plain language, the path to reintegration in the Church for the remarried is a path than can sometimes take a long time. But if we spare ourselves all that, it gives rise to more harm than any good obtained from a quick and easy blessing.

Do situations also occur in which you advise people to divorce?

Yes.

Yes?

Yes. Rarely, but yes. A separation. The Church does indeed provide for the possibility of a separation. It is there in canon law, and the Apostle Paul writes about it. This is a legitimate possibility. It becomes complicated, then, with a remarriage.

But advising two people to part, in a so-called judicial separation, is sometimes really the only possible course.

But is divorce then not the consequence of this?

It does not have to go as far as divorce. It can also be a separation recognized by the Church. It does not have to come to a civil divorce.

But there are situations in which you would have some understanding even for a divorce?

I can manage to be understanding in very many cases. Nonetheless, one has to say that the speed with which divorce is undertaken nowadays is dramatic.

3.4. Burning Questions: Where Does the Path Lead?

Whether it is celibacy, the place of women in the Church, or the Church's sexual morality, ultimately the argument is very similar. Many people are waiting for something to shift, for the Church, too, to have new responses to changing circumstances. Time and again, we finally end up at the point: How contemporary, how modern, and how flexible can the Church be? Or should she be that at all?

She should be herself. That means, she should take the gospel as the standard. I will give you an example. I visited a parish, and as happens at nearly every parish visitation, at some point when you talk with people the subject of remarried divorced people comes up. Someone addressed me rather aggressively and asked, "Why is the Church so hard on people who are divorced and remarried?" And I said to him, "Do you think it is pleasant for us priests, us pastors, to have no solution? I think we have Jesus to thank for this difficulty." And then I simply told him what Jesus had said: "For us, of course, what Jesus said is binding", and then I quoted to him, "Whoever divorces his wife and marries another, commits adultery." And at that moment he turned quite pale. And suddenly we were in another dimension. That passage struck him. He became aware of what he had known for a long time, "I have committed adultery!" That truth really shook him. That was his situation. I would not be a good pastor if I were to pass that by, since only the truth sets us free.

The other side of this life situation is that one can fall in love again, one does enter into a new relationship that perhaps has precisely this valid and binding nature. That simply takes place, every day, thousands of times a year. Even human relationships can be a mistake, people can grow apart, find someone new, love again. The Church cannot, after all, bypass this fact and behave as if all that did not happen. Without wishing to disregard the pain of a separation—there may also be a thousand reasons why a new relationship is right and good.

That is all correct, but no doctor, if someone came to him with a comparable health problem, would say, "We will not do any medical history now. We will not look at your case history but will simply ignore all that, and I declare you healthy, and you can simply go on living." No good doctor would do that. A case history is obviously part of any good treatment: "Are you aware of why this has come about?

What is the basis of the new relationship? Are you building on top of ruins, or are you leaving a house that is only half arranged in proper order when you move into the new house?" That is pastoral care. And if I do not undertake that, I am not a good shepherd.

If someone can say, after the five-point program mentioned before, "By any human standards, with all human imperfections, we have really reached a point at which we can declare: 'We have dealt with all this, we have done what we could by way of reconciliation, protecting the children, caring for our former spouse' "—then we can really take the next step and think about how full integration into the Church again might look.

Nevertheless—back to the question of how open, how ready the Church should be for new paths?

She should be open to what are truly new paths. What is often loudly demanded has to be looked at closely to see whether these are in fact new paths.

But new life-styles and forms of family life can be regarded as a fact today. They are simply a fact. Without judging them right now.

But without any evaluation at all, it does not work, because situations do precisely have their value. One thing is certain: if the Church in every case immediately follows the social trend, then she will very quickly become superfluous. If she does not maintain a certain tension of being different, of not conforming, she will also become completely uninteresting.

But if this being different takes place at the very high price of losing faithful and thus ultimately reducing the social significance of the Church!?

At the high price of losing faithful whom she would probably, however—indeed, certainly—lose anyway by complete conformity. For if the salt becomes "stupid", as it says literally in the Bible, "if the salt becomes insipid, then it is no longer good for anything." And Paul says, "Do not be conformed to this world." A Church that is no longer any different is uninteresting. Parental authority that is not also a source of friction is no authority at all. And a Church that is not also a source of friction is of no interest. Giving one's blessing to anything and everything can be better done by society than the Church. It has its rituals for that in the "yellow press", in the tabloids. We do not need the Church for that. Nor do we need a "star priest" for that, who approves all the doings of the in-crowd. Nothing comes of that.

Mother Teresa demonstrated that most impressively. In exactly the same way as Jesus himself did, because she always got through to people, right to their hearts. I heard the following story from someone who often used to accompany her. Mother Teresa was met at the airport in Bonn by some German minister or other—she was a guest of the state, a big deal. She sat in the back of the Mercedes with him—the one who told me about it was sitting in the front. Mother Teresa put aside the small talk at once and talked to the politician about his family. After three or four words, the minister's tears were flowing. She had really moved him, and they were no longer the great Mother Teresa and Mr. Minister, but two people meeting each other; and at the end of that meeting the outcome was what Mother Teresa always used to say, "Whenever someone leaves me, he should go away more comforted than when he came."

You should go away more comforted than you were before. That is exactly the point, or the criticism, of people who say that the Church does not offer them this comfort. The Church is not there for them. That is precisely what many people sorely miss, that the consolation does not apply always and for everyone, because there are so many situations in life for which the Church makes exceptions, in which she says, "No, not you."

Already with Jesus, this thing with consolation, is mixed. His approach to people is sometimes very hard, so that one is immediately afraid: How can he be so hard? There is the well-known story of the Syro-Phoenician woman, thus a pagan, who beseeches him to heal her daughter, and he takes no notice of her, does not once look at her. Then the apostles come and say, "Give her what she is asking for." So they have some sympathy for this woman, though somewhat mixed sympathy, for they say, "She is crying after us." It is unpleasant for them. I often think that is exactly the situation we have today. The media is crying after us: "The Church is so lacking in mercy. Give them, finally, what they are asking for!" Yet Jesus endures the tension. It does not happen right away, there is a way to go yet. And he takes no notice of this woman. What happens? The disciples ask him, "Give her what she is asking for, she is crying after us." He takes no notice of her, does not favor her with a glance. Then she comes and falls to the ground in front of him and beseeches him yet again. It is becoming more and more dramatic. He simply takes no notice of her. And then he says to her, because she is giving them no peace, "I have come only to the children of the house of Israel."—Only to the Jews, not to you pagans.—"It is not fair to take the children's bread away and throw it to the dogs."—Dog of a pagan. It could hardly be more inhuman. Words that seem full of contempt!

Fine, but how should we understand that?

The following now happens. The woman says to him, "Lord, you are right. It is true that it is not fair to take away the children's bread and throw it to the dogs. Lord, you are right. Yet even the little dogs get the crumbs that fall from the table." Then Jesus says to her, "Woman, your faith is great. Go, your daughter is healed." That means he has endured all this tension really in order to draw her out, to challenge her. And I often say that to our priests and pastors: Have we understood what Jesus wants of us, here? Not giving in to everything immediately, but first looking to see, "Where do you actually stand? What do you mean? Do you want Communion, for instance, simply because other people also go up, and you are embarrassed not to? Do you feel socially excluded? Is that it? Is that what this is about? What do you really mean?" That is real pastoral care.

Yes, and of course there is a certain span of time between immediately giving in and holding out forever.

The parish priest who wrote to his congregation, "With me, everyone is allowed to come to Communion", was no pastor. Nor is the parish priest who says, "With me, it is only what is in the rulebook that counts." Pastoral care is something that is differentiated and personal, and the Church's basic rules were not drawn up without regard for people, but are the fruit of profound human experience. I tell all those people who moan or rail against the Church for being so lacking in mercy: Who is lacking in mercy in this society, where people have complete freedom to divorce, where there is no difficulty at all about it? At the first difficulty, people run off from each other. Who is being helped by that? The Church is the only institution in this society that is upholding the ideal of marriage.

Who is being helped, if on the continent of Africa, where one of the greatest problems—not only an exclusively medical problem, but also economic and political—is the subject of AIDS, the Church is simply not prepared to be open in the question of the use of condoms?

On the subject of condoms and Africa, I would suggest you ask the African bishops. I do not like talking about things of which I know much too little. I had a dear friend, the Bishop of N'Dola in Zambia, who unfortunately died much too young, who had a great AIDS project in his diocese. He was a really great bishop, and should have been the one to ask.

I can see you do not want to answer that. But do you understand that people do not understand that and have a big problem with it?

What I say is that certain people—I do not mean the Pope— certain people in Rome should say less, and let the African bishops say more. There are a couple of over-zealous people in Rome, who say things on this subject when they would do better to hold their tongue. We should leave that to the people on the spot, who have day-to-day experience of it. One thing is certain, and I have seen it with my own eyes in Zambia: the AIDS pandemic is an inconceivable catastrophe for the countries of Africa. In Zambia, in the year 2000, when I was there, about a thousand teachers died of AIDS. For a fairly small country, that means the collapse of the school system. That is monstrous. And we have to ask the bishops there what they suggest. The very first rule, of course, must be marital fidelity, and not prostitution at every street corner. But . . .

But life is different. There are indeed marvelous projects for AIDS orphans in Africa and even Church projects. Yet it is a fact that by making a clear statement in favor of the use of condoms, the Church could clearly alter the situation. Even in order to remain credible for people.

What runs like a leitmotif through our conversation is the point of binding commitment. Would you say, then, that that—if we were to express it in advertising slang—is the USP, the "unique selling point" of the Church? Is binding commitment also a subject that is not communicated very clearly to people?

I would take this farther with a passage from the Bible. Pope John Paul II often said: "No life is fulfilled without sacrifice." Ego-trips are not what make people happy. I, I, I—am alone in the end. And that is why commitment, binding obligation, sacrifice is the key. I experience it at a point that is difficult to express. I will put it like this: it always impresses me when I meet people who take the trouble to devote part of their holiday time to a children's camp. Those for whom it is worthwhile, a matter of course to undertake a mission for the Red Cross. Often these are people not necessarily religious or connected with any church. But they are "committed people". And I believe that gives our society some backbone. Of course, the gospel is a path of commitment.

Is your private opinion on Church-related questions actually identical with that of the Church, or are you able to differentiate them at all?

That very much depends. There may very often be disagreement on political questions, differing assessments. I agreed 100 percent with Pope John Paul II's view of the Iraq war. But whether he was always right about the bishops he appointed ... Here you can only say, "He was not infallible there." Many subjects were addressed too often for me, I will concede that. But I am not aware of any point, doctrinally, where I would have to say I am now in disagreement.

I admit that in 1968, when I was twenty-three, I had problems with *Humanae Vitae*, Paul VI's famous "pill encyclical". And that I have in fact carried this difficulty along with me down all the years. But I have always had the vague feeling that somehow there was something prophetic in it. Whether it is quite right in its specific arguments is another question; but it was prophetic. And today I see, almost with horror, that this prophecy was true. Independent of any moral judgment, we are confronted with the fact that our continent is not really assenting to its own future. And that began then, with the pill. Pope Paul VI took upon himself solitude, misunderstanding, and an incredible amount of opposition in order to declare that regardless. I do not know how I would live if I were married. I do not know whether I would have kept to that, whether I would have managed it. I would have tried. I have met very moving instances of married couples who are able to say, "We have lived like that, and still do, and it is a good thing." But I know just as many instances where married couples tell us, "It is simply not possible." But looking back today, I have to say that

Paul VI was speaking prophetically, in the classic sense of the term, that his basic approach was right—that is, that one cannot separate sexuality and the transmission of life, as so often happens at the outset: a lonely opposition to the spirit of the age. It is a hard thing, being a solitary prophet. But forty years later, we see that here was quite an essential question. What does the transmission of life mean?

Whenever I find it difficult to understand something in the Church's teaching, I have become very cautious about saying, "That is nonsense." Karl Rahner once said to us young theologians—I was about twenty-two or twenty-three—"Whenever you do not understand something in the Church's teaching, do not say in advance, 'That is nonsense', but say, 'Perhaps there is something in this that I do not yet understand. I will leave the question open. I will stay open, intellectually and in my heart to the possibility that something will yet be found there for me.'" I must say that what Karl Rahner said at that time, in 1967, is still with me today: there is a great deal still to be discovered.

As the former Federal Chancellor Sinowatz has said, "Everything is very complicated." So it is the same for religion, is it not?

It is quite simple and very complicated. Yes, and it is a good thing that time and again we are prodded into reexamining the quick and easy answers. The quick and obvious answers are not always the right ones.

3.5.   Criticism and Self-criticism

Cardinal König once said that the Church must be self-critical and ask herself how so many of these failures of communication can come about. Is there enough of this self-criticism in the Church? From the outside, one often has the impression that no notice is taken of critical voices! What about self-criticism in the Church?

I would like our social institutions to produce as much self-criticism as the Church does. It starts with the Bible. There is no more self-critical book than the Bible. Show me a story in the literature of the world in which a people allows itself to be criticized by itself so mercilessly and relentlessly as the Jewish people in the Old Testament. If you want to write a handbook of antisemitism, then you need only reach for the Old Testament. What the prophets "declared within" their people then, all the criticism God leveled at his people—they are reproached for being stiff-necked and stubborn—it is all in the Bible. It is appalling. And then take the New Testament, written by the apostles and their pupils, and who comes off worst in the New Testament? The apostles, who wrote it. Just imagine that! Who would dare to write about themselves the way the evangelists wrote about Peter? Peter is the leader of that association!

God commanded that people, his people, to be self-critical from the beginning; and that is why I believe there is no better school for self-criticism than the Bible. As if God were constantly holding up a mirror before you, "Yes, look in there"—and then God says, "And I like you in spite of that. You are infinitely dear to me, although you are infinitely impossible." And that is why the best way of self-criticism for the Church, too, has always been reading the Bible. The Church has always done that, whenever she renewed herself: a massive wave of self-criticism! Francis, for example, criticized the Church unmercifully, but he loved her.

Are forces of self-purification also needed in the Church?

There is a book by Luigi Accatoli, with speeches and texts by Pope John Paul II, on self-criticism by the Church (title: *When a Pope Asks Forgiveness*). Many cases are listed there where the Church or people in the Church have failed in the course of history. Who would have written a similar book about the history of Austria, for instance, with self-criticism of Austrian history, of the national or economic authorities . . .

You almost sound a little offended, as if you thought the Church were being criticized too much nowadays?

The Church is very often unjustly criticized. But she is also often criticized rightly. I come back to the image of the family: nowhere is one seen as soberly as in his own family. You yourself have many brothers and sisters, you know that your own siblings are the best critics, because you cannot fool them. They have known you since you were little. That is why I believe that love is a part of criticism, accepting the other person. Then I can also accept criticism, if I know how God goes about criticizing in the Old Testament, how Christ does so in the New Testament, if I know that the criticism leveled at me springs from a passionate love, then it edifies me and does not destroy me.

It is interesting to observe this physiologically: if children are constantly being criticized by their parents, they build up defensive attitudes, and that can lead to a complete withdrawal; those are survival strategies; I have to protect myself against criticism that hits me, so to speak, in the heart, that destroys me. Then you have to defend yourself against that, and that is why I also understand the reaction of many in the Church—and I often have the same reaction myself—whenever an unjust criticism is shown, of closing up and saying, "That is really unfair, I am not going to let that touch me." But if I know that my parents and my brothers and sisters love me and truly accept me, then I can also accept criticism from them. Then it is even good for me, because it helps me.

One of the great difficulties about criticism of the Church is that it is very often loveless, and the Church does not deserve that. If I look at the sweeping criticism of the Church, on one hand, and, on the other, all the good things that happen in our parishes, the effort people make, how committed they are, I find that simply unfair. So one ought not to criticize. The way that, a little while ago, an artist said on Austrian television that the Catholic Church was the greatest criminal organization in the history of mankind, then I have to say that I do not accept that criticism, because it is either stupid or malicious—or both.

How does the Church deal with criticism from within her own ranks?

As well, and as badly, as other people do. I have written into the mission statement for the Archdiocese of Vienna this sentence: "We tell each other about mistakes and learn from that, since we regard them as an opportunity for learning." That is a noble principle. Who dares to tell whom about his mistakes? Who dares to tell the bishop, if he or she is convinced he has made some mistake? What signal does the bishop give that he is grateful for criticism? How is the criticism expressed? Is it expressed judgmentally or as a help? These are all questions about our style of dealing with things in the Church. And I think the gospel is very clear about this. In the eighteenth chapter of Matthew's Gospel, Jesus gave a clear rule for the community on how to proceed. He did not write, "Well, the first thing is to inform all the journalists." No, he said, "In the first place, talk about it in private; go to your brother and point him in the right direction. If he listens to you, you have gained your brother. But if he does not listen, then call three or four reliable people, and talk with him in a small group. If even that does not help, then tell the congregation. And if he will not accept it then, let him be considered by you as a Gentile." That means, separate yourselves from him. We usually do it the other way around. First of all, the media are informed, then the parish is upset about it, then the parish council finds out and chatters about it, and the parish priest hears about it last of all.

Is it something for confession, then?

Absolutely. In the confessional, Saint John Bosco (d. 1888) once gave a woman who had been spreading gossip the penance of carrying a basket full of feathers—chicken feathers or duck feathers—up to the church tower and leaving it there at the top. So she carried this basket of feathers up to the tower, and the next time she went to confession, Don Bosco said to her, "Well, now go up the tower and fetch down the basket of feathers." Then she said, "That is impossible now, they have been scattered in all the wind." And he said, "As you see, and it has been the same with your gossip. You cannot put it right again."

Chapter 4

What We Would Like
from the Church

4.1. A Church for Feeling Good?

From a survey of young people from fourteen to eighteen years of age, on what they would like from the Church: for example, a "more comfortable", "warmer" Church. What could that mean?

I can imagine that a little, if I think about a neo-gothic church in Vienna like the Votivkirche or the large Gürtel churches. They do seem cold, especially since they are not much frequented. If I imagine the Altlerchenfeld church, that magnificent neo-gothic church with its famous frescoes, forty thousand Catholics used to live in that parish. On Sundays there used to be one Mass after another there, completely full. Today, five thousand Catholics live there, of whom 3 or 4 percent go to church. So one can imagine how lonely you feel in that church. Of course it is not very comfortable. If I visit a Russian Orthodox church, with its icons and the singing—perhaps that is something that appeals more strongly to our feelings. If I think of Saint Barbara's, the little Greek Catholic church in the Postgasse in the inner city, with those marvelous chants in church Slavonic, the iconostasis, the incense, the candles . . .

Do you think in fact that this wish refers only to physical surroundings?

It probably means more than that, but I have to respond with a question to the young people here. In my conversations with young people, I am always telling them what I expect from them. We live in an age in which people give top priority to expectations. What do I expect from the federal chancellor, what do I expect from the government, what do I expect from the state? The question, "What do I have to do?" is rarely asked.

What I expect of young people is that they should bring some comfortableness with them. There is not any ready-made nest. Their parents have provided them a home, hopefully a comfortable nest, but then comes the age in life when you have to start building a nest yourself. Even in the Church, you cannot remain in infancy all your life and say, "Make it comfortable for me." Who does that? Should older people do that, or the parish priest? Who does it? That is a rather exciting challenge, and I have by all means come across young people who are making the Church comfortable in that sense—that is, they are enlivening the Church with what they bring to her. I am certainly aware that this is asking a lot of young people, whose connection with the faith is slight, who even from home get very little connection with it. How are they to bring that into the Church? Yet there are instances, and it is possible. I find it especially with young families. Young people between fourteen and thirty are for the most part not to be found in parishes.

Young people certainly have ambitions to provide the Catholic Church with a new spirit: it is advertised with slogans like "spirit is sexy", and rock Masses are celebrated. Does that please you?

I have only once celebrated one of these Masses, with smoke and spotlights and so on. I was very sceptical; it went on for a long time. There were certainly over a thousand young people taking part, and they saw it through to the end. There were quite intense moments of silence and, then again, explosive moments of music and enthusiasm. It impressed me. One thing is clear to me: that cannot be our usual form of worship. Yet we do also have festivals in the Church, which are not everyday events, but special times. Why not? And besides, the slogan "spirit is sexy" was a response to the German slogan, "stinginess is . . ."

The advertising slogan, "stinginess is sexy", which has by now become outdated, since even the electronics firm that used it in its advertising has turned to new methods and slogans in its publicity.

". . . sexy", yes. It was deliberately chosen to counteract that. I then got strongly worded letters of protest from people who said, "How can anyone say something like that?" If you then explain that it was a counter-slogan to "stinginess is sexy", then perhaps they can understand.

At the same time, subjects are being addressed that convey a different image of the Church. People are talking in a very open and liberal style in Internet forums about contraceptives and sexual morality. Are these deliberate developments or subversive tendencies like you get in every large group? Has the Church arrived at today there, or would you say that was going too far?

Perhaps the Church has arrived at yesterday, then, since anyone who is trying to be too modern is usually left behind by the next modern thing. The question is not whether one is modern or not but whether one takes people seriously, even young people in their situations, and whether one takes them seriously enough to contradict them.

I believe the crisis that fathers are going through, above all in my generation, the '68 generation, is dramatic, because we wanted to be brothers and not fathers. Children and young people, however, need fathers, with whom they can come into conflict and have confrontations. Sigmund Freud is no Church Father, but he saw many things quite accurately. The father represents the principle of reality. Reality is relentless. If I run up against a door, the door is real. I can deny it, but it is there. The sexuality that a young person experiences in coming to physical maturity, in his sexual awakening, also has its reality. Confronting young people with this, so that it is not arbitrary whims that rule them, is a hard process, and that should be the father's task: being the tree the young stag rubs up against, the force against which one can measure one's powers. How far can I go? What is "too far"? Where are my limits? Where are the other person's limits? If one does not make available to young people this link with reality, then one is not helping them toward mature relationships and adulthood.

But that must also hold true for the Church. That realities are simply there, irrespective of how one deals with them. That it is simply a reality that young couples have sex before getting married. That it is a reality that young women use contraceptives nowadays. That is simply all lived reality today. Whether you like it or not, it happens.

Every parish priest lives with that, and every congregation knows that 90, 95, or 99 percent of the people who are married in church are already living together. Nonetheless, the Church persistently stays with the fact that there is something different and that it is good to remember this. Just like tiresome parents say, "nevertheless . . ." Then perhaps the time comes, when one says in retrospect that one's parents were not altogether wrong. You do not agree with it, you fight against it, okay. But it is important that someone says, "nevertheless."

It is not right, because living together is not something free of obligations. That does not mean that earlier lifestyles were better. In the past, boys from a certain social class were sent to particular houses to get their sexual experience and to hold out while waiting for marriage. That is just as problematical, or perhaps even more so. I am not trying to say that the state of things in society in the past was better. But reminding people that there is something like an obligation, a reality that for the most part we do not live up to, that is basically the case with all commandments. I know that the Eighth Commandment is absolutely right, that we owe one another the truth, we ought not to lie to each other. And nonetheless I have to confess, every time, that I have not been so strict with the truth, and here I exaggerated something, and there . . . , and so on. I know that there is, thank God, this little warning voice that is not confused by the spirit of the age, saying, "Nevertheless . . ."

Do many of these things weigh so heavily on people only because the Church makes them into sins?

I do not believe that at all. I believe most people know quite clearly, in their innermost heart, what is right and what is not. But their minds are put at rest by social conventions. It is generally taken for granted today that you have to have had sex by the age of thirteen or fourteen. Do you have to? Is there not a dictatorship of public opinion, a dictatorship of approval and the mainstream, a dictatorship that forces young people into behavior patterns about which they will later say, "Why did I not fight against that? Why did people not tell me? Why did no one help me to resist?"

I am wearing an armband that the young people from the Philippines gave me at the great European Youth Day, here in the summer, and on it there is, "hundred percent pure". They gave it to me, and I put it on. I know that my heart is not "hundred percent pure", and I am sure that many of the young people, too, do not manage to be "hundred percent pure". But I was very impressed, I was flabbergasted, when those young people renewed their promise: We choose life. I would say that is a good example of being anti-trend. We are not going to let anyone dictate to us that this must be. And I believe that also offers a certain incentive to young people. I found that at the World Youth Day in Cologne, at the big meeting of Austrians. One may, say, of course, that there was a little bit of peer-pressure there: "Who will promise to wait?" Out of a thousand young people who were there, a good half raised their hands. Whether they succeed or not is another question, but that as young people they actually say it makes sense to take a different path.

Does the Church not simply risk her credibility time and again, with her rigid attitude in these questions and expose herself to the criticism of living in an ivory tower? We sooner or later have to accept what is real. If plans and reality do not correspond, then the plan is wrong, people say. The loss of credibility is after all a very high price to pay! The loss of that sense of being someone to whom people can go with their actual worries and troubles; where many people say, "Well, they have no idea at all what I'm talking about", "They have no idea how things are for me"?

I think a priest who is living with his congregation in a quite normal way today knows all that very well. He is not blind. He can see how young people in his congregation are living. Many of them come to terms with it in a rather resigned way. And many parents too, who are living in very similar circumstances, simply live with it. "Okay, that is just the way it is today." Those are today's times, and many parents even react aggressively if anyone criticizes that, because basically they are helpless. Even though they sense that their thirteen- or fourteen-year-old daughter is not ready for sex yet. It is too soon. She is physically ready, but not mentally. This is not the time yet. They would need time to "go with each other". That is what people used to say, "going with one another", experiencing things together, but not yet short-circuiting it all by going to bed together.

And yet it is still the better way to say, well, if so, then the girl, please, ought to take contraceptives or, if so, then they should, please, use a condom, and without having the feeling they are doing something wrong!?

Do you really believe that it is the Church that produces the guilt feelings here? I am fairly sure that many have a suppressed feeling of guilt in the depths of their heart, for the body and soul are quite precisely aware of what is happening. I say little about this question of "Should we, or should we not with each other"—and so on. I say to young people, Have you really listened to your heart? Are you free enough even to say, "No, that doesn't suit me"? Are you behaving like this because there is pressure, because you would feel silly in front of other people if you could not say, "Me too"? I believe it is more important to listen to one's inner voice, to one's heart, and to have the courage to follow the heart, and not "that's just what is done these days." And I am sure that for many young people it would be nicer if they were protected by a certain social barrier from taking that step too soon.

Do you not think it is far more probable that then thousands of young people would no longer ask you, the Church, for advice at all?

I know that.

Because in fact young people believe you are clueless in any case.

I am also aware of that, that people do not ask the Church about things—or in very few cases. I hope there are enough sensible adults to give young people different advice from what our '68 generation did, to have the confidence to strengthen the powers of resistance. We are going to need people in our society who are capable of saying No. Saying No against the trend, against the mainstream.

But that is exactly what the '68 generation wanted to do.

Yes, and they have become the mainstream. The Church today is in the happy situation of not being mainstream. She is able to register a protest and say, "Do not go with the flow; swim against the current. Construct an alternative culture." I find that with young families; it is absolutely great when you take part in a meeting of young families like just this summer in Pöllau, where there were three or four hundred young couples with children. They deliberately intend to follow a different path from that taken by the mainstream of society. They live in this society, but they say Yes to life, they say Yes to fidelity. And when you experience the joyfulness and liveliness of such a gathering of young, religious families like that, then you have to realize, the future is here, and not with our self-actualizers, who are "lonely surfers".

The sound of your voice changed, with the word "self-actualization". Is "self-actualization" really a bad word for you?

Not in itself, no, since, philosophically speaking, every being is trying to actualize itself. The snail is trying to be a snail; the bird, a bird; and the man, a man. There are vital forces moving us to do so. In the case of men, there is the little difficulty, in contrast to snails and birds, that they also have to do it deliberately. And that is why they are in a somewhat more difficult situation with regard to actualization, because with us there is the additional factor that men can be selfish and then become closed in on themselves and, thus, quite the opposite of what was in fact intended.

Do many people attribute too much importance to self-actualization as a goal in life?

I believe that not a few relationships are destroyed nowadays because someone suddenly says, "That does it, now I want to actualize myself." But in the end, the "lonely fighter" is for the most part also a lonely person.

4.2.   Voluntary Celibacy

A second big subject on the wish list of young people is the question of celibacy, which gets people particularly worked up. Last December, in the Vorarlberg, there was the case of a priest who concluded his sermon with the words, "I am going to be a father." The entire congregation stood behind him and demanded what many people are demanding, that celibacy should be negotiable in the direction of being voluntary.

It is understandable that that makes a difference to many people, because questions of relationships always touch people, and especially the parish priest's relationships. A congregation looks to its parish priest, who presides over it, is the role model, the pastor of the flock. Every step he takes, his every action, is observed. You can imagine how much talk there is in almost every parish about the presumed or actual relationships of the parish priest. If a woman stays ten minutes longer in the rectory than expected, the great machinery of suspicion is already set in motion. Where does he go in his car? Whom does he see? Is he perhaps having an affair after all? Does he have a girlfriend, or even a boyfriend? I believe there is not any parish in which there is not that kind of talk. There is hardly any parish priest who is not supposed to have children. And then we always get statistics, alleged statistics: 30 percent or—I do not know—40 percent of priests are living in long-term relationships. I always ask, then, "How do you think you know that?" And when you investigate more closely, a great part of it is supposition, suspicion, and so on. Does he have something going with his housekeeper? Does he have a girlfriend?—and so on. We all know these discussions, and of course when they concern a priest they are somehow more interesting than for other men.

Being unmarried is always an annoyance, of course. It triggers suspicions—is he unable to? Does he not want to? If she or he remains unmarried, have they been left in the lurch? Have they been unable to find anyone? Or, what? For someone voluntarily to renounce the active practice of his sexuality is absolutely unthinkable in an over-sexualized era. Either he is ill or he has anyway, or ... People simply cannot imagine it. Then there is always the simple solution when a problem arises somewhere: let the poor fellows marry. Suddenly, marriage is now the universal cure-all. Apart from that, hardly anyone gets married nowadays. Church weddings have decreased drastically, and even civil marriages; people live together. Sixty percent divorce rate in Vienna, and then marriage is supposed to be what is prescribed for lucky parish priests?

This is about celibacy being voluntary and, thus, about the possibility of marriage. The case in the Vorarlberg, like many of these stories, has raised these questions: this man was a good parish priest whom everyone loved, someone who was there for them, who was responsive to the concerns of the people—why should he no longer be that now because he has a child?

Let us now assume that he was a married priest—we have some in the Archdiocese of Vienna, the Greek Catholic priests who are married, who are my responsibility, and who have families. In the Eastern tradition, married men can become priests—that is what we must say to be more accurate—for it is just as strict in the East: when someone is once a priest, he can no longer get married. That is equally true for the young priest in Feldkirch in the Vorarlberg. According to the rule that holds throughout the Church, at least for Catholics and Orthodox, the rule of the Eastern Church, once someone is a priest, he can no longer get married. But married men can become priests. I am shortly going to be ordaining a married man who has four children.

He used to be an Evangelical pastor and has become Catholic along with his whole family, and the Pope has given permission for me to ordain him. He will continue to be married and have a family and will be a Catholic priest. But if his wife should die, then he cannot marry again, because a consecrated person cannot marry; but a married person can be consecrated.

The simple answer is, "It is very complicated." For, first, it is not simple for any person, married or unmarried, to integrate his sexuality. I know so many married people, from confession and from pastoral work, from conversations, who had every assumption that all would go well, and they still could not cope with their sexuality, with all the dramas and difficulties associated with it. The unmarried state, as provided for in the Catholic Church, is only comprehensible if you understand it on the basis of Jesus. And sometimes, I say in prayer, "Dear Lord Jesus, you were a man, you were a youth, you were a grown man, and even if you are God's Son, you still had a body, you had a sexual nature. You dealt with it in a manly way, you were truly a man. That is how we meet you in the Bible, in the Gospels. You were not some little weakling. You were truly fully human, a real man, indeed. How did you do it? Help us, show us, how does it work?" And then when I look at the priestly models offered to me, I have to realize that it does work. It works with God's help; it works if you have a great passion for God and a great passion for man. Then it really does work. But if one is constantly halfway, with loopholes, detours, and compromises, then halfway things result, which make nobody happy. But it is the same in marriage.

Do you mean that voluntary celibacy would be a kind of halfway thing?

No. Voluntary celibacy is a whole thing if it is lived wholly; and it is a halfway thing if it is lived halfway. And a marriage is a whole thing if it is wholly lived, and it is a halfway thing if it is lived with infidelities. And fundamentally, everyone knows that in his innermost heart. Perhaps we do not always manage it without any compromises, yet we know that those compromises do not make anyone happy, nor were they intended. I know some marvelous people, like our Maria Loley, for example, who has lived all her life unmarried. What that woman has done for people! Was she unhappy? She did without having a family, she did without getting married, but she did not do without loving. She lived love fully. She did not enter a married partnership, but she was and is a loving person. It is still possible.

Clearly, it is possible! And no one is criticizing that. No one is saying that priests should now be forced to marry!

That is very good, that we are not being forced to marry. I am very grateful for that.

But somehow I gather from what you say that in the near future there might be room to negotiate in the medium term?

Well, you see, it has long been negotiable for me because that is not an issue for me. In the Archdiocese of Vienna, I have married priests and unmarried priests; and I know that there are very good marriages among the married priests and very good unmarried priests; and I know that in both groups there are priests who find it very difficult. Where the marriage is not going well, or where they cannot come to terms with being alone. I do not expect everything will be perfection in this earthly life. It is not. Either way it is a struggle. What does a married man do when his wife falls ill? Or a married woman when her husband is ill, and she has to live for years in marital fidelity with a very seriously handicapped spouse? That happens. Are people any the less human on that account?

Do you believe that the crisis of celibacy, to use the striking phrase now in vogue, and the crisis of marriage have some connection with each other?

Absolutely.

Because with both it is a matter of a binding commitment.

Esteem for marriage always goes together with esteem for celibacy. You can trace that through the whole of Church history. And I can show you communities, among the new communities in the Church, in which both are flourishing. There are many priestly vocations there and families with many children, good, vibrant families, and one contributes to the other, they strengthen each other. But in a society hostile to children, sexuality becomes so absolute, so isolated, that people wonder, "What does a man do in a parsonage without any sexual activity?"

But what do you say now to the Catholics in the Vorarlberg, who go to church and are furious?

We have always had cases like this, even in my time in office, exactly the same sort of situation. Then I go into a parish like that, talk with people, and say, "This is like a case of divorce. This parish priest has violated his marriage, for he had made a promise of fidelity, and you were the spouse.

He promised publicly in front of everyone to live unmarried, so as to be wholly for Christ and wholly for you. He did not manage that. We are not throwing any stones at him. We are not entitled to, but this is like a divorce. A promise of fidelity has been broken here. It is very painful. He now has the consequence of that, and may they be happy together; but it is a breach of fidelity that was promised."

You have to speak plainly about things. Nobody forced him to do that: I was not forced to become a priest. One of the conditions for my becoming a priest is my being free. Just as in marriage—if I was forced to marry, the marriage is not valid, and if I was forced to be ordained and that comes out, my ordination is declared invalid. So of his own freewill and knowingly—and you cannot say that at twenty-six he did not know what he was doing—he took that path, and he broke his promise, yes. That's it. And we are so—hardhearted, a good many would say—that we say, "Okay, you have taken this step, we respect you, and we also respect the fact that you are drawing the consequences. We are drawing them with you. And we thank you for your service and regret very much, before the whole parish, that you are going. Go in peace!"

4.3. The Place of Women in the Church

The next point on the wish-list of young people in the Church: women should be given the same status as men. They should be able to become priestesses or even pope!

I can say here, quite simply and plainly, that will not happen, because the basic constitution of what Jesus founded has parameters. Jesus gave it to her to take with her, and the Church is not authorized or competent to change this fundamental constitution. That is to say, it was men whom Jesus called to ecclesiastical office. He in no way discriminated against women—on the contrary, he exercised an openness toward women that was almost offensive in Jewish circles. There were women among his disciples. They traveled with him all the way from Galilee to Jerusalem, they supported him with their money and resources, but he did not give them any office. All around them, that would have been quite natural. There were priestesses in all the pagan religions. He did not do it. I do not know whether the Holy Spirit will one day lead the Church in a quite different direction. But as we see it now, that is constitutive for the Church.

This is an interesting case of limits. Our era does not accept the limits. Konrad Paul Liessmann wrote an article a little while ago about limits, about how important they are in life. Setting boundaries in education, between countries, and not least, perhaps even first of all, the limits of our body, our skin as a boundary, so that we do not slip away. Without boundaries, there is no identity; and without boundaries there can be no encounter, since an encounter can only take place between two beings who are circumscribed. And whenever two entities share a boundary, they encounter each other, for better, for worse. The Church says that Jesus set a boundary here. One chafes against a boundary. Why is that not possible? Why am I not allowed to leave my wife?—after all, Moses allowed it! Jesus says, "That is right, Moses did allow you to do that, but it was on account of your hardheartedness; it was not like that originally. This is the boundary."

But at the same time, we also live in an age in which boundaries are not unmovable and in which we are also very glad that a good many boundaries no longer exist or that boundaries have even fallen.

It is a good thing that the Iron Curtain has fallen, and it will be good if it falls in our minds and in our hearts, as well. We are always having to overcome limits in approaching one another, in being open to what is new and strange, yet nevertheless we shall always need boundaries. That is a fundamental law in anthropology. Boundaries are a necessary condition of life. The question is, of course, whether these landmarks, these boundary posts, are unmovable, or are they culturally conditioned? A good many say that this is a typical cultural boundary from Judaism, patriarchy, and so on. The Magisterium of the Church says this is not a cultural limitation; rather, this is something Jesus laid down.

Are there actually sometimes boundaries like that or dogmas of the Church where Christoph Schönborn is privately in disagreement with the Cardinal?

I have to admit that I have not yet found any—perhaps I will stumble across one sometime. I am always coming across doctrines with which I have difficulty, but then my approach is first of all to I say "Perhaps there is something here I have not yet understood." And that is how it is also with the question of drawing this boundary—men, yes; women, no—with regard to office in Jesus' community, in the Church. Here I say, that still strikes me too. I find that is not so easy to swallow.

On the basis of our current understanding, I too make a practice in the Church, where I can, of course, of giving men and women equal rights. I have women in positions of leadership in the Archdiocese of Vienna—our finances, our accounting, our school system, and our business office. They are on full equal footing with the male leaders. I am completely in favor of equal rights there. My mother was the sole female manager in her firm and was clearly paid less than the men, although she was bringing up four children on her own. I regard that as scandalous. For that kind of thing, we really should be out on the barricades; there we have to fight for equal rights. But here it is not a matter of rights but of a mission that Jesus gave to his community to take with it. Not everyone has the right to celebrate the Eucharist, but only those who are ordained. Those who are not ordained are not thereby being discriminated against.

But would it not have been possible to negotiate with Jesus on this question?

It is a bit difficult to ask him . . .

Is that not often the problem with questions of belief?

I sometimes think that, too. "It would be nice, Lord and Master, if you could sometimes give us rather more direct instructions." There are enough of those so-called private revelations, men and women who say, "Jesus told me such-and-such"—I am always very sceptical then and prefer to look up in the Gospels what Jesus said and to listen to the experience of the Church and the saints. I am rather cautious about that.

Are you really quite sure that all the Church's interpretations are what Jesus intended them to be?

I am not sure about that, especially in secondary matters. I am not sure that he really intended everything in church furnishing to be as it is, and I feel myself quite free in that area. The cardinals' robes, for instance, were certainly not invented by Jesus.

And this, by the way, is the last point on young people's wish-list: the Vatican should make its finances public, and the pope ought not to be elected for his lifetime but should be able to be voted out.

That second question is an age-old question, hotly debated even in canon law: What do you do if the pope goes mad? What do you do if the pope becomes a heretic? Can he be voted out then? One great theologian of the twentieth century said that you are then allowed to pray for him to die. In view of his illness, Pope John Paul II—so I hear, I have no evidence for it, but I hear this—set down written, internal instructions on how people were to act if, on account of his illness, he became incapable of exercising his office. And then when he lost his voice, right at the end of his life, this question became quite acute. Is he still able to govern? And then those who shared the responsibility said that as long as he understands everything that is said, and as long as he can respond in writing or by signs, he can govern. That situation lasted only ten days; if he had lived longer, the question addressed here would certainly have come up. Then he would not be voted out, but an interim governing body for the Church would have to have been organized until his death. It is astonishing that this has practically never occurred in the long history of the popes. Popes have always died at the right time, and I know of no case in which a pope became incapable of exercising his office for any length of time.

What do you think about making the finances public?

There is no problem there: they are public. Anyone can read them on the Internet. I have the financial statements of the Vatican sent to me every year—they are public.

A favorable financial statement?

The Vatican's balance sheet has improved in recent years, because they took some economy measures and budgeted somewhat more judiciously. The Vatican is now in the black, for the first time in a long while.

Time and again, whatever point people are criticizing or what ever they would like from the Church, it always comes down to this: What has to stay? What stands the test of time? Where must the Church change? Is there a list on your side, something like a list of priorities, the most important matters, an urgent "to do" list?

Things that are not a matter of faith can of course be discussed. The question of celibacy is not a matter of faith. And it is discussed, and on that particular question, the greater part of the worldwide Church shows that it is clearly in favor of keeping celibacy. Both in Asia and in Africa, where having unmarried priests is certainly very difficult and where there are also many practical problems. But the African bishops, for instance, are convinced that with married clergy things would certainly not be easier—more difficult, if anything—because of the whole clan system. There would be far more of what we had for centuries, so-called nepotism, coming in. A parish priest, and even more a bishop or a cardinal, having to take care of all his nephews and nieces and having a whole swarm of his relations around him, all wanting to have a nibble at the priest's income or his privileges. Then he would have to see that his nephew got a scholarship and his niece a job, and so on and so forth.

That is negotiable, and people do discuss it. There is no problem about it. But I am very sceptical or cautious about the probability of any change here, because a change would be very complicated. Yet it is not to be excluded. Other matters are not negotiable. We cannot, for example, in order to accommodate the Muslims, dispense with saying that Jesus is the Son of God. That is not negotiable, because it is the core of our faith. We could discuss the exercise of the papal office. Should it be shaped this way or that? And Pope John Paul II invited all the Christian Churches to say what they thought about it. But what is not negotiable is that there is an office of Peter, of Peter's successor. That was instituted by Christ.

So that means that all matters that are not questions of faith can be changed?

All matters, that are not part of the Church's infallible teaching on faith and morals naturally lie in the sphere of things that can be changed. The Ten Commandments cannot be changed. There can be discussion about question of whether or not the Fifth Commandment, "Thou shalt not kill", applies in the case of self-defense or in the case of a defensive war. There is intense discussion about the case of the death sentence. But the Fifth Commandment as such cannot be called into question. The question is, simply, what falls under the Fifth Commandment?

Is there anything like an agenda, a list of priorities, for the negotiable questions?

Not that I know of. There are questions that come up naturally, because an emergency situation or new factors arise. The questions concerning bio-ethics have only been asked in recent years because there was no biotechnology before that. And new answers must be found there, but the principles are the same. The question then arises, "How do the basic principles need to be applied here concretely?"

Chapter 5

What Is True, and What Is False?

5.1. Religion and Morality

We have talked a great deal about the separation of religion from politics and about how these two are then connected with each other after all. Does politics actually need religion, or does it not simply need morality?

It needs morality, because every aspect of human behavior needs morality, and politics does not need a morality that is any different from that needed by other aspects of human cohabitation. There are not different kinds of morality for economics, for the family, and for politics. There is only decent and unseemly, moral and immoral. It is never good to do wrong for the sake of a good purpose. It is never good to deceive others. The Ten Commandments are comprehensively applicable. But I would give this answer to the question of whether morality alone is sufficient for politics: it is a good thing when politics and economics include a basic measure of morality. This is highly desirable. And people are clearly better off when politics, economics, and all other areas have a good, sound, full measure of morality.

The fundamental question, though, is whether in the long term any morality lacking a transcendent basis, without any basis in religion, in faith in God, without a sense of commitment to God, can be sustained. That is the big question. A good many ethicists in earlier times did believe that you have to keep religion out of ethics, out of morality. For religion, they said, carries within it the danger of doing good to please God, and not in order to be fair. I believe this is to draw a false conclusion. For the aim of pleasing God, of keeping his commandments, helps me. I am then also able to be more steadfast in the good. It is not the case that I help some person in need only in order to get to heaven; their distress, rather, addresses me directly, and I respond to it, I allow myself to be challenged by it, and I react as a human being. In doing so, I am fulfilling God's commandment, "Love your neighbor as yourself."

Can a morality without religion be maintained in the long run? There, I would reply that, from my experience, it is very doubtful whether it can last any length of time. For if our life in this world is "the last chance", and I start with the presupposition that I am not accountable to anyone other than myself for this life, not even to God, then it becomes quite easy for morality to fail. I often think that when I read the Old Testament prophets; the threat of God's judgment does us all good. Not so as to make us fearful, but to remind us that this life is terribly brief. And we have a terrible amount of responsibility in this life, and being reminded of that whenever we are inclined not to think about it at all does us a lot of good. That is why it is good when the prophets, like irksome admonishers, remind us, "Some time you will have to give an account of what you have done with your life."

You have said that the Ten Commandments hold true for everyone, everywhere, and for every profession. Are they adequate in language and content for our present-day world, with our current problems?

Absolutely. I do not know anything that should be added to them. Three commandments concerning God and seven concerning our neighbor—and they are not detailed commandments, but general ones. We can of course have endless discussions about how they should be applied. What does, "You shall not bear false witness" mean? What is a white lie? Do I have to tell everything? Do I have to tell a journalist everything she asks me? And then there is so-called casuistry. One can debate what the application of this general commandment would be like in particular cases. "You shall not bear false witness", the Eighth Commandment, holds true everywhere. And we find this is true by cross-checking it. There is nothing more painful for a person, for his well-being and his dignity, than having to say to himself, "Someone has lied to me." Honesty and truthfulness are such fundamental virtues that we very quickly realize that the lack of them is a major shortcoming.

Yes, but let us stay with lying, as the same example: we live with lies. They are all around us. And we recognize them, we expose them, when we think about it anyway. Whether it is in politics, in the media, in advertising, or in the economy. They are part of our life, and we deal with them as we do with the truth. What is the commandment "You shall not bear false witness" saying to me, then?

The commandment says to me still more clearly that it holds true universally, comprehensively, everywhere, and at all times. Why do we hide our lies under the appearance of truth? Everyone tries, when they fib a little, to represent things so that they appear to be true. Advertising lives on that; our little and, unfortunately, also great deceptions of one another live on it. It is quite impossible to sell a lie without dressing it in the mantle of truth. That is what propaganda depends on, selling lies under the appearance of truth. And prophets always had the dreadfully unpleasant task of removing this mantle and calling the thing by its name. In a Corpus Christi sermon —those sermons always have a sociopolitical touch—I once said, quoting an ancient Chinese sage, Lao-Tse, "If you want to put things in order in politics, you have to put things in order in the language." I cited one example: all of us, our entire economy, depends on autos. Yet the word "auto" is a deception we all use to lie to ourselves.

It brings many advantages, and it brings many problems—but whom are we deceiving?

"Automobile" means, literally, "it moves of its own accord." It does not move by itself, at all. It runs thanks to petroleum, the raw material accumulated in the earth over millions upon millions of years, crude oil, which we will have burned up in three or four generations. That means we have lived with the lie of the automobile for a few generations, at the expense of the history of the earth and of all people living after us. I admit that I use an automobile and that I would probably find it very difficult to carry on my ministry without using an auto at all. But the word is a lie.

You will now say—you have already suggested something along these lines—that we scarcely can live without lies. Yes, and no. We cannot help being part of a society in which we also do things we know, if we are honest, to be not quite right. We cannot get off and go to another planet. But we should at least not spare ourselves the trouble of trying to live in truth. Jesus said something that is frequently confirmed: "The truth will make you free." Sometimes we are so afraid of the truth we panic—"For goodness' sake, if anyone finds out!" Nevertheless, we know that nothing produces greater freedom than the truth, and nothing produces greater bondage than lies. Why do people talk about "a web of lies"? It becomes a network of lies, it becomes ever more complicated, until one day it no longer holds up, and then the truth comes to light. That does not mean that we expose others or ourselves, making use of truth in a loveless way. Cardinal König had as his motto a saying of the Apostle Paul, "Veritatem facientes in caritatem": "To do the truth in love." Without love, the truth is unbearable. Yet without the truth, love is hypocrisy.

Why does it not work to translate Christian commandments into everyday terms, actually to live them? One often has the impression that many believers forget, as soon as they go out the church door, what they have just heard and praised. How can I go into church, describe myself as a Christian, and then come out, and I am a manager, a politician, a journalist, or whatever, and do everything quite differently?

There is a quite simple explanation for that in the Bible. It is found in the first pages of the Bible, in the third chapter of Genesis. In theology, we call it "original sin". We are furnished with a fallen nature. A human nature that is in a fairly desolate state. That is to say, in every human being there is an inclination toward evil.

It was one of the illusions of the Enlightenment to believe that this was an invention of religion, of the priests, to keep people quiet with awareness of their sin. And thus Jean-Jacques Rousseau (d. 1778) invented the man who is naturally good and denied the existence of original sin. The results were not very happy. The French Revolution very quickly showed that men certainly do have an inclination toward evil, to a quite appalling degree. Our old brothers and sisters of Judaism talk about "Yezer haRah" and "Yezer haTov", the good and evil drives. In every person there is a leaning toward good, which is, thank God, stronger than the leaning toward evil. Being good is more pleasant than being evil. Even if the leaning toward being bad does portray being bad as something good. But this evil inclination is a burden to man from the start, and even if he is baptized, has been immersed in the baptismal water, this evil inclination has unfortunately not ceased to exist. Martin Luther said, "You have to drown the old man again, every day", in the water of baptism, and rise anew as a Christian person.

Now, does that mean that man is basically evil? That is not what the Church teaches. We are created for good and oriented toward the good. But there is this drive in us that is already perceptible in childhood. Let us observe small children. A child has a little brother or sister, and already there is jealousy. The child has not learned that; it is not the bad example of the parents, rather it is within him. Sigmund Freud described the child as "polymorphously perverse". I find that a little severe. Manifoldly perverse. But children's cruelty is sometimes horrifying. When I recall my own childhood, how I used to go mad with rage—and how much I still have to struggle with anger. Psychology cannot explain that away for us. That is a moral and religious dimension that we call original sin.

The teaching of the Church says that original sin is not personal guilt. The little child coming into the world has no personal guilt, but he has received a human nature from his parents that does have a leaning toward evil. That is why *eruditio*, as the Romans called education, is a strenuous effort to pull someone out of a condition of brutality. Education is a constant battle against the drive toward evil. And since our education is never completed, we still have to struggle against this as adults and even as old people. That is why virtues are so important.

In recent decades, people have liked to smile somewhat about virtues. They sound nineteenth-century and rather musty. Yet meanwhile, we are discovering again that virtue is what makes people good. Virtue is a good habit. If I repeatedly make a small self-conquest, if I come to my office and do not let my fellow workers see how cross I am, but overcome myself and am friendly and ask "How are you?" If I do that time and again, then it becomes a habit, a *habitus*, a virtue. And then it gets easier. Then I do not have to conquer myself again every time; I have acquired it. That is why the basis of every proper human life, and most certainly every Christian life, is the acquisition of virtues.

Religion and morality used to be closely intermeshed, and nowadays we do not know what we should take as our guide, what is right and what is wrong. Who are the moral authorities today? Whom can I ask for advice—a lawyer, a psychologist, a nuclear physicist?

People. Wise people. Mankind has always known that: "Consilium semper a sapiente perquire", it says in the Bible. "Seek counsel always from a wise man." Do not go to a fool. There are great scientists who are outstanding in their own field but who are fools and have no wisdom. And there are quite ordinary people who have not had much education but who are very wise. So that means, "Ask a wise person!"

How do I recognize one?

In the Bible there is a whole literature about wisdom, the so-called "Wisdom literature". It includes the book of Wisdom, Sirach (or Ecclesiasticus), Proverbs, the Song of Songs, and Ecclesiastes. There is a wealth of literature there concerned with this question. Where do I find wisdom? Among wise men. How do I know that someone is wise? Not those who consider themselves wise or who say they are wise, but people who have proven themselves in life. How do I recognize people who have proven themselves in life? By a certain intuition. People who do not consider themselves more important than they are. Who are simple. People who do not look down on others. And for the most part, too, people who have been through a considerable amount. Very often, people with a deep faith. What a country and a society need, in order to discover values, is to look at the wisdom of life—not at what is currently in fashion, but at what is valid.

Has the path you have followed in the Church, your examination of the faith, made you wiser?

I certainly hope so. The wisdom of the Gospels is incomparable. There are words and actions of Jesus that are so wise that you have to say, "Yes, that's it exactly." There are certainly wisdom teachings in all religions. There is certainly profound wisdom to be found in the sayings of Buddha, in Confucius, in the great masters of religion, in the great philosophers. But I believe there is only one about whom it can be said that he is wisdom itself. Jesus is not merely a wise man; he is God's Wisdom who lived among us. That is why I think that there is no better school of wisdom than the Gospels.

5.2. Virtues

The difficulty starts at the point where virtues begin to conflict with other demands. So, is it clever for me to be honest? Can

absolute honesty be reconciled with fairness and considerateness?
What part does justice play? Everyone is equal before the law.
Must they, therefore, be treated the same? How do justice, equality,
and motivation relate to each other? What kind of taxation system
is just? What unemployment benefit? Is it more fair to have the
rate at which things are taught in a school class suited to the more
gifted pupils? Or those less gifted?

What do compassion and solidarity mean? How do perfor-
mance orientation and solidarity relate to each other? What place
do you assign to tolerance, and how far should it go?

Virtues always run into difficulties. That is true even of
natural virtues, not just of Christian ones, because the imme-
diate payoff seems to be on the side of the vices, but not if
you look closer. Not for nothing popular wisdom says, "Honesty is the best policy." If I am dishonest in business relations, then perhaps in the short term that will be successful,
but in the long term it ruins my trustworthiness. In business, solid partnerships are always still the most successful,
where a handshake can be trusted. I will choose a workman upon whom I know I can rely. And one who does a
botched job and deceives me will not be working for me a
second time. But the workman whom I know to be rock-
solid, who is honest I will employ again. That is the way
everyday life works. Every business relationship is based on
people trusting each other. And I will not take someone
for my business partner if I know he is not trustworthy.

Let us make it concrete: Can absolute honesty, for example, be
reconciled with the command to be fair and considerate?

All virtues have a common measure by which we assess
whether they are truly virtues: love. Justice without love

becomes inexorability. Knowledge without love runs the risk of becoming craftiness, or diplomacy in the worst sense. Fortitude without love becomes recklessness. The same is true of values. You can find value without love at the bank, as stocks and bonds. The measure for all value and the measure for all virtues, is universal: whether they are shaped by love.

I would rather talk about virtues than values, because "value" is an economic concept. It offers a material analogy. "Virtues" are ways of acting, and that is why in their case it is not so much a question of their value as that of proving themselves in life. That is why I like to say "virtues" rather than "values". That is likewise true of the example you mentioned, honesty, sincerity, and . . . what was the other thing?

Fairness and consideration for others.

Consideration for others. That must be measured against love. An honesty or truthfulness that hits or beats someone over the head with the truth—that cannot be it. Only love can really make truthfulness a virtue. If I say to a sick person, "Your illness is fatal, and you only have three days to live", and communicate that to him with clinical coldness, so to speak, that is loveless. I must look at what his situation is like, so that he can grasp it. I have to be alongside him in order to be able to tell him that. The same holds good for fairness. Considerateness should not go so far as to become cowardice or pretense or dishonesty. Love is able to expect a lot of someone because it is done in love. And it will find the right measure, what the other person can bear and sustain.

How does that look with regard to justice, equality, and motivation? If we look around in the world, what is the measure for equality and justice?

Equality concerns our dignity first of all. All men are equal in dignity. Even the worst criminal is always still endowed with the dignity of being human. And that is the reason why I am ever more clearly and decidedly opposed to the death penalty.

But equal dignity does not mean equality in all areas. Talents are not equally distributed. That is why I am very sceptical about the concept of comprehensive education, unless this is clearly counterbalanced by differentiated assistance. Someone who is musically gifted must be handled differently from someone who is mathematically gifted. A child who is a low achiever needs to be encouraged differently from a high achiever. You cannot measure everything with the same yardstick, and you should not want to treat as equal things that are not equal; to be fair, you must treat unequal things in an unequal way.

Yes, but the critical question of political orientation is then, yet again: Should we go by the weakest member or the strongest?

We have to do both. The strongest member, in education, needs particular encouragement, because a particular gift is involved. It would have been a bad thing if Leopold Mozart had not given his son particular encouragement. He saw that quite consciously and said, "God has entrusted such a unique talent to my care, and I would be sinning if I did not promote it." But you would not treat someone completely lacking in musical talent in the same way as Mozart.

Saint Catherine of Siena (d. 1380) once had a vision—this is cited in the Catechism—when God said to her that he deliberately created people to be as unequal as possible: "I have given many gifts and graces, both spiritual and temporal, with such diversity. . . . I have willed that one should

need another. And so that you may be constrained to practice charity toward one another, so that no one may say to
another, 'I do not need you'". That is de facto the case. I
would be completely lost if I had to fly an airplane myself—
and the pilot would probably be fairly lost if he were put at
the altar and had to celebrate Mass. We need each other. I
cannot repair my own shoes. Thank God there are shoe-
makers. Nor can I solve my electrical problems myself. I
am constantly dependent on other people. Because we are
completely unequal. We all have the same dignity. We are
all human beings, but we are extremely unequal.

Compassion and solidarity: what do they have to say to us today?
How important are they?

Compassion is already programed into people by nature, or
by the Creator. There is a well-known example of that from
psychology. You look at a child, and the child's face, this
rounded shape—this has already been studied in neurology,
in research on the brain—triggers a positive reflex, a reflex
of caring attention. We spontaneously turn our attention to
a small child, as we do not do with adults. Konrad Lorenz
(d. 1989) and behaviorial scientists have done research on
that, and research on the brain also studies which synapses,
which combination of neurons, are functioning here. Sympathy, then, has a physical, vital aspect first of all, and we
have to say, thank God our nature is programed in this way,
so that we do not immediately see an enemy in everyone
we meet. I wince whenever I see someone else in pain.
Why is that so? I am currently reading a fascinating book
by the neurophysiologist Joachim Bauer, *Warum ich fühle,*
was du fühlst? (Why do I feel what you are feeling). Research
on the brain has discovered, with respect to the so-called

mirror neurons, that I immediately feel a kind of pain myself whenever I see someone else with an intense pain. This mirror effect shows that we are oriented toward sympathy.

This does not, of course, remain in the realm of instinct, but it has to be tended and cultivated, like everything else and requires us to overcome any antipathy, which may be very strong. I have to work on myself here. I find someone unlikeable. I have to work with that colleague. I cannot just stick with my primary reaction of antipathy here, which—whatever its reasons may be—is preprogramed. I have to work on my sympathy. That may go as far as it did with the little Saint Thérèse, Thérèse of Lisieux (d. 1897). She found one sister in her convent particularly unlikeable. Someone who was difficult in general. The others also suffered somewhat from her. Thérèse made a special effort to be patient and loving toward her. She also wrote in her autobiography that one sister there was so difficult and that she had to make an effort herself to be sympathetic and friendly. And after Thérèse had died and her autobiography had been published, the sisters naturally wondered, "Who was this sister she found so unlikeable?" They all knew right away who was meant—only the person concerned did not know, because she always thought, "Thérèse was always so nice to me that it cannot have been me."

We are able to work on our instincts, too, and go beyond them. The same is true, of course, of solidarity. Solidarity is in the first instance a vital and instinctive feeling, the group feeling. We know about that from the most varied phenomena in soccer stadiums; that vital solidarity when the "Mexican wave" runs round the entire stadium. Why does the individual know that he is going to take part in it? It is completely instinctive. The same way that birds do their incredible group flights, and starlings do the most fantastic loops in group flight. It is instinctive. Solidarity has a vital basis. But the vital basis can also become a danger. I will never forget an experience I had at school, in grammar school. I think it was in the fourth grade, which was situated in a barrack. It was unbelievably primitive in the years just after the war. There were three classes in that barrack, and there was a kind of swinging door with glass panes. In some tussling during the break, someone banged against one of the glass panes with his elbow, and it broke. We were a group of about ten lads, there. Suddenly, a second boy, as if he were intoxicated, broke in a second pane, and a third boy another one, and within seconds all the panes of glass were smashed. Then we stood there as if horrified. Now, what was that about? It was a group reflex, a completely senseless, uninhibited destructiveness. Those sixteen windowpanes were gone. In a matter of seconds. That was a key experience for me of how group solidarity can also lead instinctively to evil, to chaos. So that even the primal, vital feeling of solidarity needs to be cultivated and domesticated.

All demagogues make use of the instincts of solidarity to inflame. Hutus against Tutsis in Rwanda—that went all the way to genocide. It was whipped up, stoked up. Suddenly, solidarity becomes murderous frenzy. Then, there is overcoming this elemental solidarity by genuine virtue. A quite staggering example of that comes from Rwanda, from the time of the genocide. There were about forty seminarians in a seminary for priests, a mixture of Hutus and Tutsis, and the rebels came along and demanded that the seminarians should separate themselves into tribal groups. That clearly meant that some were going to be killed and the others would survive. All forty refused to separate. And all forty were killed. There you can see how solidarity moves into another dimension, how it became solidarity in a fully human sense and not merely in an instinctive sense.

A brief aside on the subject of soccer. I have read about a religious group in Korea for whom playing soccer for several hours is part of their ritual, because the game of soccer and the public's enthusiasm for it have a religious power. Can you understand that?

I am probably the least qualified person to say anything about soccer, since I was the worst soccer player in my class. There were two of us, the biggest one and the smallest, and I was the tallest. We were always the two left over at the end when the teams were picked. Then the two team captains would say, "Now are you going to take Schönborn or are you going to take the other one?" So I was never very good at soccer. But I do know that there are some very good soccer players in clergy circles. There are even clergy soccer championships. There was a clergy international match between Austria and Hungary. I think Hungary won.

It is certainly not just in a stadium, at big matches, that soccer represents something sacral, a sacred ritual. It has a great deal to do with discipline, with solidarity, with team spirit. It is a fantastic school for learning to act together and react to one another, to adapt oneself to each other. You are completely dependent on each other. That in itself is something marvelous. It is in some sense a model for how things ought to be in society, with people really showing perfect teamwork—as they say. During the European championships in our country in 2008, there are going to be some Church initiatives to provide a religious dimension to this great event. It was interesting to see how many players in the soccer world championships made the sign of the cross before starting to play.

Back to virtues—although they are really not that far removed from sport: responsibility and sense of duty.

I would place something else before those. What people used to call "embarrassment", the sense of what is appropriate. There are certain things one does not do. There can be a lot of hypocrisy about this, yet it has great significance for a society. When embarrassment disappears, then much of the fundamental structure of the society goes with it. When there is no longer any common code of behavior, then the value of the social standards has seriously declined and demands concern today. What is happening to embarrassment?

And then we are at the next higher step, sense of duty, sense of responsibility. There is a lot of talk about rights today. Duties are far less often mentioned. There is a great debate about the whole area of human rights. To what extent do we also have to formulate human duties? The Gospels, the Bible mention many such duties. The Ten Commandments are fundamental obligations for man. If I am not aware that I have obligations, no society can survive in the long run. I am thinking of an area where this is especially and painfully evident, the social benefits provided by the state. Do I use only those social benefits that I really need, or am I getting all I can out of them? Even when I do not need them? That is the question of embarrassment. One ought to feel embarrassed about claiming some help one does not really need because one can well afford to make material provision for it oneself. A great deal of any society's welfare depends on whether people deal responsibly with the freedoms offered by that society, such as the benefits or services offered by a welfare state.

A quite different but closely related area is that of responsibility in the workplace. Economizing certainly helps us nowadays to be frugal and responsible. That is sometimes taken to excess, and the drive to economize becomes so relentless that it is taken to the limits of what is humanly possible.

When those businesses that are making the biggest profits shed most of their employees and expect those who remain to produce just as much.

That is a situation which, in the long term, burns people out. I think that here again, that is a responsibility that falls on someone. To what extent do those with the most responsibility still have control of what is happening? To what extent are they not themselves the ones pushed and shoved and constrained by their shareholders, by the share prices, by the valuation of their business, who then have to pass that pressure on down? Where can we truly find accountability in management nowadays without this kind of pressure?

Upon what should the laws in this area be based? Does the highest value, the justice of a law, really have to be measured according to how great the potential for abuse is?—Instead of directing it according to what is really needed?

That is one of the fundamental questions of democratic society. How great is the individual's power of self-discipline, so that one can more or less dispense with any measures of protection against misuse? Here we have to say first of all that there will always be a danger of abuse as long as we are human beings. One of the most dangerous perspectives is the one that forgets about original sin. In the discussions about unconditional basic income, one of the people involved said to those advocating a basic income that they were not taking original sin into account. They do not figure that people are inclined to abuse that, for example, by being lazy or by refusing to work, and so on. Therefore, there always has to be a certain degree of sanction in our laws, because without any sanctions at all we all too easily slip into abuse. If I know there will certainly not be any police on the roads, and if I know there will certainly be no radar traps, then am I certain to keep to 80 miles an hour on the freeway, as allowed, or would I not, after all, run up to 100 miles an hour?

And what do you do?

I keep the cruise control strictly to no more than 80.

Yes, the cruise control. No, I would never do anything else either, unless I had a police escort. That has already happened. And then, you can drive at 125 on the freeway.

That example shows us that we need sanctions, the warning finger which reminds us, "Careful, there is a punishment for that, there is a penalty." That helps the embarrassment factor. Of course, it is nicer when the embarrassment factor is so taken for granted that sanctions become unnecessary. Yet laws do need to have them, otherwise they have no bite to them. But laws should not be made up of the sanctions but directed toward the real matter. In the case of the most recent example, however, of mothers whose children are not covered for child benefits, the question is: Were there gaps in the law itself, so that the implementation of it led to this loophole? That is what I suspect, and that is why a revision of the law was necessary.

What does fidelity mean to us at a time when 62 percent of marriages in the city end in divorce?

That is what we all long for most deeply. I believe there is no way people are more deeply disappointed than by breaches of fidelity. That is incredibly painful because fidelity is the basis of all human relationships. That is true, first of all, in the family. As a child, I rely on the fact that my parents wish me well. Nothing more dreadful can happen to a child than to experience rejection by his own parents; that his parents are not faithful to him, which means they are not permanently well-disposed. Why is it that nothing hurts so much as a breach of faithfulness in a relationship, in love? Why is it so dreadfully painful for one when he is cheated by a business partner or someone with whom he has shaken hands on a deal, or maybe even signed a contract, in business, in some company or enterprise? You wind up some business and then discover, "He cheated me." That gets to you really deeply. And that shows that we are strongly dependent on being able to trust each other.

We are right in seeing mistrust as something deficient. There is something lacking in the humanity of someone who is deeply mistrustful. He has not been given the gift of trusting and, thus, experiencing fidelity. Vice versa, it is one of the loveliest things in life—and I am very happy to be able to experience this—when friendships last for decades. If I am able to say that I have some friendships that have lasted since my childhood, already over thirty years, that is wonderful. If I imagine that if one of these friends had deceived me, that is, acted against me, stabbed me in the back, it would have been enormously painful. And I think that what is most profoundly characteristic of the biblical picture of God is the word "faithful". God is faithful. We find that in the Old Testament on practically every other page. In one of Paul's epistles, it says, "God is faithful. He cannot deny himself if we are faithless; if we are faithless, he remains faithful, for he cannot deny himself."

Does the great number of relationships breaking down give you food for thought? And what conclusions do you draw from that? What needs to happen? What should we do? Why is it happening?

I see it as a great catastrophe. It means, in fact, in each case that children experience the breakdown of their parents' relationship. I believe that in order to discover one's own identity, as a man or a woman—in childhood and in youth—it is indispensable to experience how one's parents behave toward each other. If children never experience the spark of love between their parents, the erotic spark as well, if it crackles and tingles a bit in the good sense; experience their fondness for each other and intimacy, the fact that it is something living—if they never experience that, how are they going to learn it? How are they to learn that a partnership is something living, something exciting? And how are they going to learn that you work your way through crises if they have not experienced the way their parents help each other through? That is why a divorce is a drama for the parents, but much, much more so for the children.

That is a very bleak prognosis.

A very bleak prognosis for a society in which so many young people have not experienced a successful partnership between their parents. It is quite dramatic for society. It is traumatic.

Does that inevitably mean that these children will grow up with a certain kind of inability to form relationships, or may it also mean the opposite? That for this next generation, with all the children of divorce, the permanence of a relationship will have a very great importance?

That may be. We can hope so. Statistics, unfortunately, tell us something else. Thank God there are exceptions to the norm. There really are situations in which the next generation says, "We do not intend to do it like that", and they are successful. Yet statistics are unequivocal in saying that children from broken marriages are clearly more likely to get divorced than those from marriages that stay together. That makes me greatly concerned.

Are not the failures and, above all, acceptance of these failures, as well as mercy toward those involved in these failures, among our most important tasks? And also among the Church's most important tasks?

Provided we recognize that it is a failure. Mercy cannot mix with self-righteousness. If anyone goes into a new relationship convinced that only the other person has made mistakes, without even the beginning of self-criticism or an awareness of his own fallibility, then mercy has very little foothold.

Jesus always offered people mercy after confronting them with the truth. He says to the woman at the well of Samaria in the midday heat, after talking to her a little while, "Go get your husband!" Then she says, "I have no husband." And then Jesus says to her, "Yes, you are quite right. You have no husband, for you have had five, and the one you are living with is not your husband." That is the breakthrough. "There is someone here who has told me everything I ever did." She runs back into the village and tells it to all the people. "There is someone who has told me everything, but he said it in such a way that he was not condemning me." She brings the whole village out to Jesus. Without the truth, mercy has no point of contact. If I cannot see where I have failed, God cannot grant me his mercy. Self-justification and self-righteousness are the only things Jesus was really hard on. "Woe to you Pharisees", he says. "You are like whitewashed tombs." He uses his most severe words for them.

To conclude on the subject of virtues: Do you really believe that in our world of today, according to our current maxims, someone can be successful and virtuous?

Absolutely. I am firmly and solidly convinced of that. We see it in little things as well as in big things. People trust a business if they know it is reputable. We do not need to dwell on banking scandals in our country. When managed in a dubious way, then it cannot be trusted. Virtue is not an outmoded attitude that makes you old-fashioned and rigid; rather, it is the one thing that makes it possible for us to live together at all.

In order to deal with what we call "original sin", virtue is the first thing. Virtue is, so to speak, in the language of physics the *negentropy* of daily life. *Entropy* tends toward letting things slide, letting oneself go, not living in a virtuous way. You give vent to your ill humor, follow unrestrained passions, and so on. The negentropy, the counter movement to that, is in my struggling with myself and overcoming myself in little things, day after day, and gradually that becomes second nature to me, and I observe that life is nicer and much more pleasant when I am friendly and honest, when I have some backbone. That does not mean that it gets easier, but it is finer, more meaningful, and more fulfilled.

Since that effort is often unsuccessful, a second thing is indispensable: forgiveness. If there were no pardon, mercy, or forgiveness, we would be in a bad way with our evil tendencies. We are not locked into our evil inclination. We can say, "I'm sorry." I go back, in a sense, to the point at which I took the wrong direction and say, "I want to change this. I will go in the right direction." That is what is called a new leaf, contrition, starting over, making a new start. And that is only possible, if the all-embracing dimension of mercy exists. If I stood face to face with a God who only weighed and measured precisely, who kept a precise record of all my bad behavior, my missteps, my vices, and billed me for them down to the last penny, then it would look very bad for me. But I know I can trust in his mercy, because he knows of what we are made. I can say, like the Prodigal Son, when he thinks to himself, "Father, I have failed, I have sinned, take me back again." These two elements together make it possible for us to lead a happy life, despite our evil tendencies.

Let us take a concrete example: if I have a job as a manager, as chief executive of a major corporation, and I have to lead this corporation through a difficult period economically, then it is my job to make sure that it makes a profit and not a loss. I may possibly be faced with the question of whether I should, whether I must lay off five hundred people, whether I MUST give them notice in order to maximize the corporation's profits? And at the same time, I am someone who thinks along Christian lines. How can I take my Christian thinking as the basis for business or financial decisions? Or, does my life as a Christian take a short break?

There are so-called practical constraints that we meet in every job. Certain things are possible or not possible. You cannot escape these even through virtue. If a business cannot survive economically without reductions in personnel, then you are confronted by the question of either nothing at all or layoffs. Yet it is also seen—I could mention a whole series of examples—that there are by all means other ways that are more human, more Christian, and perhaps even more economically reasonable.

I mention one instance that is only a little thing but still a good example. In the Austrian Post Office, one department was being closed. One of the staff members of this department, forty-nine years old, was called to the director and was told, "You can go to this particular public health officer, and you will be given early retirement for health reasons." Whereupon he said, "But I'm as sound as a bell." And then they made it clear to him that he had no other choice. At that time, he was preparing to become a permanent deacon, and he reflected, "This is actually ideal. I will be given a pension by the Post Office; I am forty-nine, sound as a bell, and I shall be able to give all my time to the Church." He talked it over with his wife, with friends, and with the deacons' formation group, and came to the decision, "I will not take it. I cannot tell lies and cheat at the expense of the general public. Even if it is a deception that is practically commanded." And then they said to him, "Right, then you will have to put up with going to another department, and there you will earn a good deal less. And your pension will also be correspondingly less." He said, "I accept that." Naturally, people talked about what had happened. At his ordination as a deacon, in Saint Stephen's Cathedral, many of his colleagues were there. And it became clear to him, and to us all, that by taking that step, he gained in credibility as a deacon. Even though he earns less now and has a worse job; but his truthfulness was worth it. His life is more credible and, thereby, also more contented.

I mention that as a very small example. There are of course more important people who are confronted by decisions like that, as you said, and behave differently. It has always been people with backbone who have changed the course of history. I could give you two or three examples of businesses where I know they were successful through good leadership, with a real solidarity of the workforce, with economizing that had an effect even on people's pay, but with real solidarity, both to keep people on and to keep the business going. I believe we are now in a situation economically, not only where rethinking is becoming an urgent necessity, but where more and more people are in fact beginning to rethink things. It cannot be that the news that five hundred people are being laid off immediately drives up the market value of a business. Yet I do admit that for someone with economic responsibility, this is an extremely difficult situation, and if he is trying to live that out as a Christian, it is certainly more difficult still.

But that is only on one level, asking, "How can I reconcile economic responsibilities and decision making with my Christian values?" Is it not so in most cases that maximizing profits, fame, power, and money are put in the place of religion? That the economy has long been our substitute for religion?

Yes, but the one little difference is that substitutes for religion do not hold up. That was already clear in the Old Testament of the Bible. Idols are nothing. It is idolatry when money is given first place. Idols cannot help us. They are will-o'-the-wisps. And in fact we are also finding that this extreme globalization, this extreme ordering of things according to shareholder values, does not work in the long run, because essential parameters are being forgotten or suppressed. So-called human capital, the loyalty of people, their affiliation with a business, the experience people have gained in that business and which they put at the service of the business in their own work—those are important values. And if those values are being systematically neglected, then sooner or later the company will pay the price for it.

5.3. Renunciation

Is the influence of religion decreasing on account of our material affluence? Is wealth the natural enemy of every religion?

Perhaps superficially. Of course, we all run the danger of becoming satisfied, when things are going well and we regard that as being a matter of course. People say, "Need teaches you to pray", and it is true that experiencing our dependence, helplessness, vulnerability, often makes us more alert to the fact that we depend on God. Yet I am convinced this is also possible in good times. This is a question of reason, alertness, and vitality, and I can maintain that even in good times. There are simple recipes for this. Gratitude. I have to be grateful, every day, that things are going so well for us. Then I have done what is essential. I have to remember, every day, that it is not a matter of course that we live in peace. If I remind myself that it is not a matter of course that I am in good health, and then I am thankful. An American uncle once said something to us children— the famous rich uncle from America: "Never take anything for granted!" Those words made a deep impression on me. Nothing should be taken for granted. If I have that attitude, then I can be a joyful, thankful Christian person even at times when things are going well, for religion does not have to disappear on account of affluence. I would say, rather, that becoming irreligious in times of affluence is a sign of folly in the biblical sense. It is foolish.

Do you see a distinction between the faith of simple people, perhaps even of poor people, and faith in a situation of affluence?

Well, we are still in these parts in a situation in which affluence is more widespread than it ever has been before in history. We can say with great certainty that in the history of our country, there has never been such affluence as there is today. And that is something very gratifying. We should see that as entirely positive. It is good when things are going well. We just need to be aware that things are going well for us. It is foolish, shortsighted to overlook that. If we then begin to grumble and moan and be discontented, without seeing how many good things we have.

There must have been some reason why many founders of faith communities or religious communities always lived in a very modest way, in simplicity, even in poverty. So does faith need—does it

need, in order to get down to the wellspring of human existence—
the experience of poverty, modest circumstances, simplicity, frugality?

Of simplicity. In the founders of religions, and quite uniquely in Jesus Christ, we see inner freedom. Saint Teresa of Avila (d. 1582) said, "If it is partridge, let it be partridge. If it is lentil porridge, then lentil porridge." When things go well, we are grateful; when things go badly, or if we are living through hard times, we do not let it get us down. This inner freedom, I believe, is the real fruit of faith, and luxury brings with it the foolishness of believing we need all that. I can recall a relative from Prague, who like us had lost everything and who came to the West in 1945 as a refugee. Then she married a very wealthy American and had a very good life. What made a great impression on me as a child, as a young person, was the fact that she was always overflowing with gratitude. Again and again, she would say, "Can you imagine me, so-and-so from Prague. That poor woman, and how well things are going for me now. That is really marvelous." If you live with this kind of attitude even in wealth, then the danger that Jesus saw in wealth is not so great.

Particularly for prosperous people in our affluent world, it makes a
big impression, though the experience can also be extreme, when
they actually meet poor people—whether over here or on other
continents. You almost have to take care not to become cynical,
because you very quickly get the impression that they are much
happier than we are. If you think that over, it is a cynical reflec-
tion, since many of them do perhaps really live with more inner
freedom and are thus more open and carefree—but the objective
adverse effects are still there! Why should someone who has no
water or who has to walk miles to get to water be happy? Money

does not make you happy—we know that. But certainly, neither does poverty!

That is something that has always struck me on journeys to Africa or Asia or Latin America. You see far more people laughing than you do here. That gives us food for thought, of course. But saying, on that account, that they are happier? They have to content themselves with their destitution because they have no other choice. It is not for nothing that countless people from these very poor countries try to emigrate to the islands of wealth in order to find better living conditions. I can understand those young Africans who do everything they can to get to Europe, because they simply have "no future". Our stronghold of affluence in Europe, where we are better off than ever before in history, attracts poor people from the poorest countries. And that brings me to a point that also came up a while ago in the question of the economy.

Whenever we hear, these days, the figures for what is being spent on armaments in the world each year. I heard yesterday that the thousand-billion limit has been exceeded. A thousand billion dollars are being spent in the world on armaments. That is so outrageous, such a scandal. When you know how a few of those thousand billions could be turned into a worldwide emergency fund, so that a billion people would not have to live on less than a dollar a day. Then you certainly have to say that this injustice in our world is—as the Bible calls it—a sin that cries out to heaven. And I believe that the conflicts we are living with at present have to do with the fact that these injustices that cry to heaven cannot simply continue. If things are not deliberately changed by the rich countries, then they will definitely find the poor demanding their rights, and they will not be able to refuse them.

Perhaps no one really wants to change it. Let us stay for the moment with the example of an injustice that cries out to heaven, the effects of which we are constantly experiencing, and nonetheless we are incapable of changing it. Another example: we know what is needed, and we cannot implement it in a binding way—because there are always other, bigger, and more important interests. We all know, all over the world, about the scandal of the arms industry and the money spent on it. We all find that scandalous, and yet it is simply not possible to change it. Are the people who have to make these decisions all without morals, without religious beliefs? Do they have no faith—is it not really cowardly to say, "There are practical constraints"?

Certainly, from the perspective of history, we have to say that too much money has always been spent on armaments in comparison to other expenditures. When you see what medieval towns spent on their fortifications, those were gigantic sums for the time. Yet in an age of total communication, of complete simultaneity, as we have nowadays, in an age where the means should be available to alleviate the worst emergencies, one cannot help but say it is a scandal all the same. Even though we can state the reasons for much of it, because the political and economic dynamics simply work that way.

I know a country in Asia where there has been civil war for twenty years—Sri Lanka. People who know the situation very well say there would have been peace long ago between the Tamils and the Sinhalese if the warmongering economic interests had not stirred up the war again time after time. That is utterly scandalous. It is not simply a law of nature. And then, time and again, there are people who have the courage to say, "That cannot go on", who stand up against it, perhaps at the cost of their lives. Bishop Oscar Romero (d. 1980) in El Salvador was someone like that.

Thank God, there have always been such people, and we have to hope that policies will be shaped by people like that. And if there are courageous people, then the policies will be courageous.

That is the best chance, and also the greatest risk, that policies are shaped by people.

That they are shaped by people who, for instance, as is the case here in Austria, were in concentration camp together and promised each other, "If we get out of this, then we will no longer do what happened between the wars in our country." And that succeeded, because there were people there who had said, "Even if we are on opposite shores ideologically, we no longer want something like civil war in our country. We want a social partnership. We want to live together with each other, because we have learned where conflict with each other leads."

Why should that not happen in the Near East, too? A solution of mutual coexistence in the region has already been almost within reach. It always depends on people, and I do not believe that practical constraints have the last word here. People change policies. People change the international situation.

Pope John Paul II changed the course of world history. Without the military, without an army. But when in 1979, a few months after his election, he went to Poland for the first time and said to the Poles that they have their own dignity, an earthquake shook that whole country. That opened the first crack in the wall. Communism collapsed, certainly, for other reasons as well; but first of all because a wave of hope ran through a whole people, hope that could no longer be destroyed.

Do you see any people at the moment who have the potential to change the world in a positive sense?

If you ask me directly like that, I see no outstanding person at the moment. There certainly are such people. And as a believer, I say that there are perhaps some in an entirely hidden form. There is an old Jewish tradition that says the world can continue to exist only because there are twelve just men. These, however, are concealed, because they are not famous people. The twelve just men. There certainly are people who by their holiness, by their prayers, by their sacrifice, and by their love see something like the invisible foundations of the world. And of course we believe in them; they are the saints of heaven.

The Mother of God has certainly often intervened in history, sometimes directly, in the past 150 years. I am not saying that lightly, now: there are very strong grounds for it. I will mention only one example. It is accepted today that Ali Ağca fired those bullets at Pope John Paul II on the orders of Andropov's KGB. What those who organized that murder had overlooked was the date. They chose the thirteenth of May. The thirteenth of May was the first day of the appearances at Fatima in 1917. And the Pope, hit by that shot in vital organs and hovering between life and death, immediately made that connection: May 13. And after he survived, he said, "One hand fired the bullet, but another hand directed it." A year later, on May 13, 1982, he traveled to Fatima, and he placed the bullet that should have killed him in the crown of the Mother of God. We are being guided by heavenly powers. It is quite certain that this heavenly direction is at work. Pope John Paul II forgave his would-be assassin and visited him in prison. The assassination attempt took place in 1981.

At Fatima, Mary had pronounced a particular message concerning Russia: Russia will be converted. In any case, that attempted assassination was a decisive step toward the collapse of Communism. With regard to the movement of history, its dramas and its catastrophes, it is brought about by people. Sometimes, too, by people who release demons. Yet it is also being made from heaven.

It is brought about by people, and also by demons in the name of the Christian faith. Is the Christian faith—or, shall we say, something disguised as Christian faith—especially suitable for hypocrisy?

Religion is very suitable as a disguise for hypocrisy. But before I go into that question, I would like first of all to speak in praise of hypocrisy. The hypocrite tries to cover himself with a garment of virtue. We have already talked about this. To that extent, the person being a hypocrite is at least attempting to preserve the appearance of virtue and making a certain bow before virtue.

Yes, but mostly in order to attain very unvirtuous goals.

That is one side of it. On the other side, Jesus probably criticized hypocrisy more sharply than anything else. Religion is well suited to hypocrisy, because people expect a pious person to be pious, and to live in a pious way. And if someone particularly emphasizes his piety, but it is being put on externally for show, then this classic case of hypocrisy is a great scandal. It was not without reason that there was nothing Jesus denounced as much he did hypocrisy, because religion is so easily misused in that way. That is why Jesus says so emphatically that one should not make a show of one's piety: "When you fast, anoint your head and wash your face, that your fasting may not be seen by men; but anoint your head and put on a happy face when you fast. Then only your Father who is in secret sees it; he will reward you." Do not seek a reward from men, rather, seek to please God and not men.

Whether Christianity is especially suited for this, in comparison with other religions, I would not venture to assert. I know many Christians who are hypocrites, sometimes myself included. I do not know the hypocrites of other religions well enough to be able to say. But one thing is certain: the corrective for this inappropriate attitude is probably nowhere so explicit as in the Gospels.

Has the gospel improved the world over the past two thousand years?

It is difficult to verify this, because we do not see how the world would look without Christianity. But one thing we can certainly say. If we are trying to work for justice: in the name of the gospel, people have achieved incredible things in loving their neighbor.

But have also done quite dreadful things; quite horrible atrocities have occurred in the name of the gospel.

Yes, atrocities have also occurred. It has become almost a ritual to stress the atrocities that have occurred in the name of Christianity or were done by Christians or under a guise of Christianity; and very often in complete ignorance of the actual history. There is one zealous author, Karlheinz Deschner, who has put together multiple volumes of material under the title of *Kriminal geschichte des Christentums* (The criminal history of Christianity), painstakingly collecting all the misdeeds of Christianity.

I will mention one example, at the risk of being criticized for that, too. In 1420, something quite appalling happened in Vienna, the "Vienna Gezerah". Several hundred Jews perished; they were driven out of the city to the village of Erdberg, and burned to death there or sent out onto the Danube in rudderless boats. Some had barricaded themselves in the old synagogue on the Judenplatz and ended by burning themselves to death in order to escape forced baptism. On the Judenplatz, at the so-called "Jordan House", there is a late medieval notice in Latin that boasts about this burning of Jews, talks about "Jewish dogs", and sees their death by fire as being in some sense a forced baptism—a staggering document of hatred for Jews in the Middle Ages, which also surrounded itself with Christian motives.

In '98 I had a memorial plaque put up on the Judenplatz. During excavations at that time, the remains of that synagogue were discovered with scorch marks from the self-immolation. I referred to that and the dramatic events of that time on the plaque at the "Jordan House". This text was discussed with the religious community, and there was only one word we could not agree about. I talked about the Christians' share of the guilt. A good many people thought one should simply talk about the guilt of the Christians. I have never seen a city, a country, or a state apologizing for a medieval anti-Jewish pogrom. The Church has done so, thanks to the great example of Pope John Paul II.

That was not just a purely religious initiative. There was a great deal of politics behind it. It concerned the Jews' money and the question of whether perhaps the Jews were coming to an agreement with the Hussites and constituted a fifth column in the midst of the city. There were political reasons for it, and religious reasons were interwoven with them. It is very one-sided always to say only "the Christians". You can of course say that they were all Christians. But these were also political and economic interests, these were the rulers of the time. And that is why it is so unjust to charge the Church or Christianity with the whole history of quiet, which is much more complex when looked at more closely, whether we are talking about the Crusades or the Inquisition. The awkward thing is, the more closely one looks at something, the more cautious one's judgment, because the things are complicated.

5.4.   In the End

How do you deal with it yourself, if you see sanctimoniousness among your flock? Do you simply accept it?

I first of all ask myself, "Are you bothered about this because you can see yourself in it, or are you honestly bothered about it?" "Hypocrite, mon frère", Charles Baudelaire (d. 1867) wrote, "hypocrite, my brother". Hypocrisy—sanctimoniousness is a form of hypocrisy—has two sides to it. Baudelaire said, "Hypocrisy is the tribute paid to virtue by vice." That is to say, the hypocrite makes an effort to appear virtuous and, in doing so, at least recognizes that it would be a good thing if he had virtue. That is to say, he still has a certain capacity for embarrassment.

Or he merely wants to appear virtuous?

Or he merely wants to appear virtuous. That is the downside of hypocrisy: putting on false pretenses, wanting to appear other than one really is. But the borderline between what is an honest attempt at preserving at least the appearance of virtue and the case where it is a matter of being seen and praised by people, for which Jesus reproached hypocrites, that line is very fine.

But that means that you appreciate the efforts made by all those who come to church?

I would put it like this: anyone who goes to church nowadays has no reason to be a hypocrite. For he is one of a minority laughed at by a large part of the population. "What, are you such a bigot as to go to church?" It might have been the case in earlier times, when everyone went to church on Sunday and put on their Sunday best, in order to be seen. That is no longer the case today. I believe the little band of churchgoers, above all in towns, come because they have honest intentions, because they are serious about it. No one has paid them to come. No one asks them whether they go to church, which would at most be derided. I do not believe there are large numbers of hypocrites sitting in church nowadays.

There is an expression that is used as an insult, "You will end up becoming a Catholic." What does that mean, at worst—and at best?

I will only talk about the best case.

You are only responsible for the best cases?

I want to see only the best possible case. In the best case, that means that someone wants to live with this marvelous community of the Church and not to cause her too much disgrace. Because I still have to say, even after sixty-two years, I know of nothing better. I have found nothing more lovely than this Church. The fact that she is imperfect is very lucky for me, since I thus have a place in her.